DISTILLING HOPE

"Stories are powerful. They teach. They transform. They make truth accessible. They open doorways to explore life in deeper ways. Veteran Storyteller, Beth Ohlsson, has provided us with a powerful work in *Distilling Hope*. These stories lead us on a path toward recovery and hope.

"You will find yourself sitting on the edge of your seat, fully engaged in each story. As you read, you will be prodded to think about your life. You will identify with characters and situations in the stories in ways that will shed light on where you are on the road of recovery. Coupled with the stories is a workbook section that will allow you to do deeper work as you engage the story where it intersects with your life. This section is well done too!

"As a pastor, I can see how this powerful work can be useful to people from all walks of life and in many settings, both groups and individuals. I am confident that this work will be another tool in helping people open doorways to hope and healing."

—Martin Hutchison, Pastor, Community of Joy Church. www.joyfilled.com Founder, Camden Community Garden, www.GrowCamden.com

DISTILLING HOPE

12 STORIES TO DISTILL THE 12 STEPS

STORIES ADAPTED BY

BETH OHLSSON

ILLUSTRATIONS BY

SHAE GEREMIA & MICHAEL FINLEY

Parkhurst Brothers Publishers
MARION, MICHIGAN

www.parkhurstbrothers.com

Parkhurst Brothers books are distributed to the trade through the Chicago Distribution Center, and may be ordered through Ingram Book Company, Baker & Taylor, Follett Library Resources and other book industry wholesalers. To order from Chicago Distribution Center, phone 1-800-621-2736 or send a fax to 800-621-8476. Copies of this and other Parkhurst Brothers Publishers titles are available to organizations and corporations for purchase in quantity by contacting Special Sales Department at our home office location, listed on our website. Manuscript submission guidelines for this publishing company are available at our website.

Printed in the United States of America

First Edition, 2017

2017 2018 2019 2020 2021 2022 16 15 14 13 12 11 10 9 8 7 6 5 4 3 2 1

Library of Congress Cataloging in Publication Data is on file and available upon request from the publisher

ISBN: Trade Paperback 978-1-62491-105-7
ISBN: e-book 978-1-62491-106-4

Parkhurst Brothers Publishers believes that the free and open exchange of ideas is essential for the maintenance of our freedoms. We support the First Amendment to the United States Constitution and encourage all citizens to study all sides of public policy questions, making up their own minds. Closed minds cost a society dearly.

All URLs in this book are being provided as a convenience and for informational purposes only; they do not constitute an endorsement or an approval by the publisher of any of the products, services or opinions. Parkhurst Brothers Publishers bears no responsibility for the accuracy, legality or content of linked sites or for that of subsequent links. Contact external sites for answers to questions regarding their content.

Interior design by	Linda D. Parkhurst, Ph.D.
Cover art by	Brian Morgante for TreeHouse Artists
Text illustrations by	Shea Geremia and Michael Finley
Proofread by	Bill and Barbara Paddack
Acquired for Parkhurst Brothers Inc., Publishers by:	Ted Parkhurst

112017

This book is dedicated to

William L. White, whose white papers defined Recovery as a Heroic Journey,

to Elizabeth Ellis who first encouraged me to tell that story,

and to all the courageous men and women who undertake the journey of recovery.

Contents

HOPE IS THE MESSAGE

That's what we storytellers do.
We restore order through imagination.
We instill hope, again, and again, and again.

—Walt Disney, *Saving Mr. Banks*

HOPE IS THE MESSAGE OF RECOVERY. In Twelve Step meet-ings around the world, people tell their stories of addiction and recovery, instilling the hope that anyone can live a sober life, a useful life, a life filled with love and joy. It is the classic heroic journey with its Road of Trials, the Belly of the Whale, the Return into the World, and Sharing the Gifts of the Journey. (Campbell, 1973) AA's first members "discovered that sobriety involved not only not drinking, it also required throwing out the old way of life—learning to follow a new map, a new way of life ... And that way of life, they discovered, could be learned and taught only through the process of telling stories (Kurtz and Ketchem, 1992, p.114)." People struggling with their addiction, be it substance or behavior, went to meetings and listened to these sober storytellers tell their stories, again, and again, and again. These stories were often full of horrific, gut-wrenching experiences that fueled an addiction and often resulted in severe consequences. But in each and every story, the hero/heroine emerged like a phoenix from the ashes, willing and able to move back into the world to rebuild their life. Our sober storyteller was proof that one can change, and life can get better.

It is an oral culture, Twelve Step Recovery. It is an oral culture thriving in a digital world. Wisdom is passed on, passed down, through the sharing at meetings, working one on one with a sponsor, talking with others on the same path. Sharing stories of experience, strength, and hope sheds light on the path. This is great for people who go to meetings and work their recovery program in this traditional way.

Not everyone seeking recovery goes to Twelve Step meetings. There are many paths to recovery, not just the Twelve Step Model. But, every path requires a new way of living that leaves the pain, shame, stigma, and failure of the past in the past where it belongs. Sadly, many seeking recovery do not have the support, the internal resources, the paradigms, the beliefs, or role models to provide the necessary guidance for a different way of life.

How do these people navigate the recovery journey? Where are the role models, the guidelines, the wisdom, the encouragement to continue the path? That's a good question. It's the question that I have wrestled with since I found myself working in the addictions field in 2000. Several years before, I became a storyteller in the traditional sense. I was encouraged by other tellers to use traditional folktales, fairytales, myths, and legends in this new endeavor.

Why? Because traditional stories all have characters that experience a dilemma, make some not-so-good choices, or have some not-so-good luck, and find themselves caught between a rock and a hard place. Then, something happens. The hero or heroine becomes able and willing to transcend the consequences and make their way back into the world no matter what it takes. If traditional stories could illustrate the recovery journey as an heroic quest, could they be used to illustrate the Twelve Steps as a design for living? Yes.

Traditional stories can illustrate the potential hazards of addictive behaviors, as well as the benefits of a different set of behaviors and attitudes. Some folktales contain constructs for persevering through pain and suffering, facing and conquering one's fears, and taking risks to love and trust. These are among the challenges one faces when choosing to abandon an addiction lifestyle in favor of a sober one. Ancient and traditional tales are useful in that they provide wisdom and model overcoming obstacles. Myths, folktales and fairy tales are infused with hope. Cultural norms, traditions, and values are illustrated and taught as they had been for centuries. More contemporary stories illustrate how to navigate and negotiate this world in which we live, and allow the exploration of perceptions, beliefs, behaviors, and consequences in a safe way. Happily, the use of story capitalizes on the way the brain remembers, indexes, and retrieves information. (Schank, 1990) It is clear from research that story is a potent influencer of thoughts, attitudes, and behaviors.

That was the inspiration behind this collection of stories. Drawing on my own experience as a person in long-term recovery, my professional experience as a drug and alcohol counselor, and my gifts as an educator/artist, I have paired each of the Twelve Steps of Recovery with a traditional story. Contained in this collection are cautionary tales, trickster tales, and inspirational tales, each chosen to touch the heart, fire the imagination, and spark useful conversation about how to live without relying on alcohol or drugs. Each version of the stories has been re-told from a recovery point of view in order to validate common experiences and introduce models for new behavior. The hope that the wounds can be healed, the soul can be soothed, a new freedom and a new happiness can be found, can be communicated through traditional stories. The power of stories to inspire change and infuse hope needn't be limited to the rooms of Twelve Step meetings. Somebody just needed to connect the Twelve Steps to stories universal stories that transcend time and place.

This book does just that. Enjoy!

Beth Ohlsson
Salisbury, Maryland
October, 2017

Each of the Twelve Steps quoted under chapter titles are used with permission from *Alcoholics Anonymous: The Story of How Many Thousands of Men and Women have Recovered from Alcoholism*. 3d ed., New York, Alcoholics Anonymous World Services, 1976

HOW AND WHY STORY WORKS

To Clinicians, Educators, Clergy, and Artist Educators:

I FOUND MYSELF WORKING AS AN ADDICTION COUNSELOR in the year 2000, in a therapeutic community contained in a local detention center. My formal training had been as a secondary theater teacher. My informal training has been my own program of recovery, which started in 1991. My newly discovered passion was storytelling. I had no idea where the path would lead and how these three things would converge. I was about to find out.

I had just left public education after twenty-five years of teaching theater. I had been at storytelling workshops with various working performers and had just begun to tell stories professionally. I was nine years sober. I needed a job. My story coach, Susan Gordon, had begun working for the local health department as an addictions counselor. Susan encouraged me to apply for a job there. This was prior to today's credential requirement, so the most important qualification was being sober. "You'll be great. They need someone in the adolescent program." I got the job, but it wasn't with the adolescents. This job put me in the therapeutic community at the local detention center. There were fifty-two men ... and me. I had little in common with these men, and had no clue how to make recovery dynamics relevant to them; much less make recovery [...]. Susan, who held a Master's Degree in the [...] c Settings, said, "Tell them stories." I wan[...] ut of your freakin' mind!" but trusting S[...]s.

I told the old stories, th[...] had loved as a child. I found new vers[...] those sto[...] t spoke to the personalities, dilemmas, [...] challenges of t[...] en. I realized that their worldview di[...] contain the para[...]s of "good conquering evil" or "money [...]sn't buy happiness" [...] "what goes around comes around." But the stories conveyed those paradigms in easy-to-digest morsels. I gave them the paradigms for sober living through story … non-threatening, non-judgmental story.

Initially, the men responded to the stories as one would expect. The stories were considered child's play and met with disdain. However, it wasn't long before the men would ask, "Are you telling stories today?" If the answer were, "Yes," the men would rush into their cells, grab their pillows or blankets or both, and curl up like children, while I stood in the center of the Block. Often they went to sleep. These men, neglected and discarded before their time, shared with me that no one had ever read to them, or told them stories. They would apologize for falling asleep and missing the story. I was touched, but still had no idea what good this was doing. I went back to Susan Gordon with these questions. She explained the "story trance" and how the story was healing on some deep level. This "story trance" is a phenomenon that occurs when the listener experiences a complete immersion into the story being told. There are observable, physiological changes in the listener as the storyteller captures the listener's attention and directs it inward. (Stallings, F. 1988) This "story trance" allows the listener to enter the mind and heart of a character, or enter a different world from their own. The experiences that listeners share as a result of this common experience of the story invite emotional growth and healing. Still dubious about all of this, I kept telling stories until I had that "Ah-ha!" moment that changed the trajectory of my life.

At one point I told "the Emperor's New Clothes" by Hans Christian Andersen, and one particular inmate had dismissed the experience as childish. I told the story to illustrate how easy it is to follow the crowd and not think for one's self, and how telling the truth took great courage. However, I have learned that what I intend and what the clients hear isn't necessarily the same. Several weeks later, this inmate was struggling to explain how he felt after responding to the aggressive and threatening actions of another. He had behaved differently, out of character, and avoided a physical confrontation, without being perceived as weak. He finally blurted out, "I felt like that little kid at the end of "The Emperor's New Clothes!" He had gotten the words he needed from the story. The members of that group session had experienced that same story, and had the same words. They now had a way to talk about feelings and experiences without being too vulnerable.

There was now a way to talk about new possibilities for responding to the world. I kept telling stories. I looked for stories that illustrated the Twelve Steps. I wanted to understand this power that story had so that I could use it deliberately and with purpose. So, I went to graduate school to study story and its power to heal. My Master's Thesis explored the use of story in addictions treatment.

Years later, while working in a women's treatment center, I told "The Monster who Grew Small," a story from Ethiopia about facing one's fears and cutting that "monster fear" down to size to a group of young mothers. Many of these women were on methadone, which is a medication-assisted treatment for opiate addiction. Methadone is often prescribed for pregnant opiate addicts as it is less harmful to the baby than heroin. It is not uncommon for a methadone-exposed newborn to require medical monitoring while the baby withdraws from methadone, which places the infant in the neonatal intensive care unit. While attending her newborn infant in the neonatal intensive care unit, a young woman was berated by one of the nurses. She shared that while the nurse was putting her down for her drug use, the story about fear went across her mind. "I took a deep breath, looked that nurse in the eye, and said, "I can't change that, but I'm clean now, and I'm learning how to stay clean. When my son is five years old, and I've been clean for five years, this won't matter to him. What else would you like me to do?" She had a different way to respond, a way that was appropriate, assertive, and positive—which was illustrated in that story.

I was blown away by her story, and the courage that she had derived from a story I told.

This was powerful medicine. I kept telling stories. Time and again, clients would reference a story when talking about a new behavior or insight. Connecting with feelings, creating community, exploring difficult topics, and making a point were easier within the context of a story. Clients remembered those stories and continued to draw strength and comfort from them, even years later. I knew this was too good to keep to myself, so I compiled this set of stories to illustrate the Twelve Step Design for Living. Regardless of the path that you may have chosen or believe in, these stories illustrate universal spiritual principles that all major religions of the world teach. Besides that, they're really good stories.

This book is the culmination of all that I hold dear—my recovery, the richness of a world shared through story, and the connections that are made as a result. What I have discovered in my own recovery journey is that I have a sacred obligation to pass on what was so freely given to me by those who came before me. I give it to you in the form of stories—stories that can be read, used, and dissected, and debated. Use the space provided at the end of each chapter to make notes, and/or follow the list of activities related to each story. Please take these stories and use them to suit your purposes, to expand what it is that you do with and for others, and to challenge yourself to work outside the box.

THE FIRST STEP

We admitted we were powerless over our addiction,
and our lives had become unmanageable.

THIS FIRST STEP has two separate and equally important components. The first part is the admission that something other than reason, intelligence, or necessity, has taken over. The second is that the addiction hijacks all other responsibilities, tasks, and commitments. What does powerlessness look like for these professionals? What does an unmanageable life look like?

THE THREE DOCTORS
An Irish Drinking Tale

There were once three doctors who had been friends for a long time … all the way through medical school, their internships, and residencies. Even though they all had different specialties, they lived fairly close to one another. Several times a year, they would get together to share a few drinks, have a good meal, and share their challenges and successes of the recent months. On this particular night, they gathered at a small tavern just out of town.

After the first round of drinks, the first doctor declared, "I have just had the most outrageous and challenging experience of my entire career! Just a few weeks ago, my wife and I were at a craft fair. It was a beautiful day, but very, very windy. There were quite a few outside displays, many of which were quite flimsy, especially given the gusts of wind blowing through the fairgrounds. All of a sudden, a gust of wind picked up a display of pottery and sent it flying towards one of the barns! When the display and the pottery met the barn, pieces of glass and pottery went flying everywhere! People were ducking and running away to avoid being cut! One poor woman, minding her own business was coming out from the barn when a piece of glass sliced off her nose! I picked up the nose, ran to the hysterical woman and got her to lie down on the grass. And right there, without benefit of a hospital or an operating room, I whipped out my Swiss army knife to find the necessary tools, pulled a thread out of the hem of my pants, and used it to put the nose back! Not only did I put the nose back, there was no scar. And she could smell. Top that!"

The other two doctors agreed that was most impressive, but their dinner had arrived, and so there was a momentary pause in the conversation. It was the second doctor who began the conversation just as the plates were being cleared. "Well, I must admit that's impressive, but ... replacing an entire eye with no loss of sight is the most challenging and difficult surgery I've yet to attempt. Just last week, a young woman came to me after an explosion in the factory where she worked. She was wearing a burqa like some Muslim women do. The burqa covered the fact that her entire eyeball was hanging out of the socket and lying on her cheek! Frankly, it was macabre. I immediately took her into my examining room, and without benefit of anesthesia or an operating theater, I reattached the optic nerve, the blood vessels, the retina, and restored the woman's sight! Not only could she see, but her eyes tracked perfectly! Top that!" Another round of stout was brought to the friends to fuel the boasting.

The third doctor slammed his empty mug on the table. "Well, see if you can top THIS! Several weeks ago, a young man came in with his hand wrapped in a towel. It was bleeding profusely all over the carpet in my waiting room. He was cradling the wrapped arm like a baby while he sobbed like a baby. He had taken the train to audition for the symphony, and he was about to miss his stop. He put his hand out to stop the door from closing, but it continued to close and just about severed his hand! I whisked him into my examining room and without benefit of anesthesia or an operating theater, I re-attached the hand with such skill and artistry that the scar was almost invisible. In four weeks, the young lad was playing the piano again. In six weeks, he was auditioning for the symphony, and tonight, tonight he is playing his first solo with the symphony orchestra. Top that!" And once again, another round was brought for the three friends, fueling the boasting.

Once the boasting was done, the arguing began. That happens when the drinking goes long. Not too long after the arguing, the daring began. And just before the words erupted into blows, the first doctor stood up, put his hand to his nose, twisted it off, and threw it down onto the table. "I will put it back on my own face in a fortnight. If you're so sure you're a better surgeon than I, let's see you do it! Cut off your hand. Tear out your eye! And put it back in a fortnight! I dare you!!!"

Another round was needed to seal the deal. And another round was required to dull the pain as the other doctors removed the agreed upon body part. They left them on the table, while the blood dripped onto the floor. The three doctors yelled for the kitchen boy. "Put these in the freezer. We'll be back in a fortnight to put them back!" they shouted as they stumbled out of the tavern. Do I need to tell you what happened to the rest of the customers at that tavern?

The poor busboy picked up the tablecloth by the corners, trying not to vomit. He dumped the entire mess onto the chest freezer in the kitchen, and returned to clean up the dining room.

When the kitchen boy went back into the kitchen, he let out a scream. "OOOOOH, NOOOOO!!!" The dog was chewing happily on the hand. The eye and the nose were gone. Panic set in.

Poor kid. It was his first night on the job, and he really needed his job. His mom could no longer work, and he had to help support his family. He was terrified he would wouldn't be able to help his family.

"Now what am I to do? Where am I to find an eye, a nose, and a hand? The undertakers? ...No, he would want to know why. Hospital? No, I could get caught by one of the doctors....Where to look? I don't even want them to come back and find that their body parts are gone forever. What will I do?" The kitchen boy left the tavern and walked home very, very slowly. On the way home, he tripped over a dead cat, and a wicked little thought went through his mind. He picked up the cat and took it home. Very carefully, he extracted the eye, put it in a zip-lock baggie, and threw it in the freezer. Then the wheels began to turn and soon, he was thinking like a rebellious teenager. The next day, the kitchen boy went to the prison and asked to see the felon who had been hanged. "WAAHHHH! That man you hanged? He was my uncle. I hadn't seen him since I was a wee boy. I need to say 'good-bye.' Would you let me see him, please?" He made quite a scene, feigning hysteria, and putting the warden on edge.

Our friend insisted again and again that he was family and he needed to pay his respects. Actually what he needed was a hand. As soon as the warden had taken him to the morgue, the kitchen boy started to wail, presumably from grief. The warden excused himself to give the poor lad some privacy. As soon as the Warden was out of sight, the kitchen boy whipped out his Swiss army knife, sawed off the hand, and put it in a zip-lock baggie, and took it home to throw it in the freezer. Now he had two body parts. He just needed the nose.

Several days later, the kitchen boy offered to help the butcher with the slaughter of a pig. Butchering is a big deal in a small country town. It's dirty and smelly and bloody, but at the end of the day, there is a great feast, so lots of people come. By the time our friend got to the farm, the hog had been slaughtered, and the butchering had begun.

The boy wasn't interested in the ribs or chops that were to come. He just wanted the snout. Carefully and as unobtrusively as possible, he made his around the farm, looking for the head of the hog. It was on the top of a trash pile behind the barn. He looked over his shoulder more than once as he made his way to that trash pile. The boy pulled out his Swiss army knife, cut off the snout, put it in the zip-lock baggie (he came prepared), took it home, and threw it into the freezer. Success! The hand, the eye, and the snout were put back into the original bag, taken to the tavern, and deposited in the tavern's freezer..

On the appointed night, the three doctors met once more at the tavern and ordered drinks all around several times before requesting the bag and beginning the surgeries. You don't think they did this sober, do you? The first doctor reattached the nose, which was really the pig's snout. He found he hadn't remembered how large and hairy his nose must have been. Considerable sculpting of the nose was required to make it sit right on his face. The first doctor was too drunk to notice that he now snorted when he laughed.

The second doctor then attached cat's eye into his right eye socket. He had to struggle to make the nerves and tendons match up. He was too drunk to notice that the eye was so small he had to turn his head to see to the right. His peripheral vision to the right was gone.

The third doctor attached the felon's left hand where the doc's own hand had once been.

The tendons and ligaments didn't align well, and the wrist was at least an inch too big. There was considerable stretching of the muscles and skin of the doc's left wrist to accommodate the hand. He was too drunk to notice that the hand kept finding its way into the pockets of others.

In their drunken stupors, the three doctors declared the bet a draw, and that they were all, indeed, accomplished surgeons who did have to work in the morning. Each returned to his abode to sleep it off. The first doctor was hung over, and therefore, late getting to his office that next morning, and the waiting room was full. Dear Mrs. Tingle had been to the market already, and had a basket of fresh vegetables and greens on the floor next to her. The smell was so intoxicating that the doctor dropped to all fours, thrust his snout into that basket, and began rooting around in that basket! There was a considerable buzz in the office, and when the doctor looked up, he had greens dangling from his lips. Do I need to tell you what happened then?

The second doctor opened up his office, head throbbing, and began to see patients. As the first patient walked down the hall to the examining room, the doc saw a white mouse race across the hall. He pounced on the mouse, stuffed it in his mouth and turned to greet his patient with the mouse's tail still moving in his mouth. Do I need to tell you what happened then?

Despite the hangover he had, the third doctor managed to drag himself to his office the next morning and begin to see patients. As soon as the first patient stood up to walk to the examining room, the doctor reached for the man's wallet. The man punched the doc and fled the office, followed by the doctor, who then noticed a pair of diamond earrings on a female patient and reached for one of them. Then he grabbed a watch from another patient. Then the doc grabbed a purse and began to run. Do I need to tell you what happened then?

Word of the doctors' bizarre behavior had spread all over the town, and no one wanted their services. With no patients, there was no income. With no income, there were unpaid rents and debts. With unpaid rent and debts came robbery. With the robbery convictions, came prison … for a very long time. These three doctors were never heard from again.

$\sim$

Discussion of "The Three Doctors" As It Relates to Step One

Consumption of alcohol, drugs, or food, as well as, gambling, sex, and shopping can escalate to the point that a person believes that he or she cannot get through the day without a "fix" of some kind. Morals, values, goals, and dreams all wither and die in the wake of active addiction. Denial of the severity of the addiction allows the behavior to continue. Then follows the inevitable path of destruction as the addiction completely takes over, dictating how one lives in order to feed that addiction. When people are confined, told how to live, when to eat, what to wear, and what to do, it is because they are no longer able to manage their lives in a manner consistent with the laws of the land. That is powerlessness. For the fortunate, the pain of powerlessness leads to a moment of surrender, a moment of clarity, when someone realizes, "I can't do this anymore." That is the beginning of the recovery. Sadly, not everyone gets there.

War stories are part of the culture of drinking and drugging. It's only a matter of time before it becomes evident that the drinking and the drugging beget problems. This tall tale captures the hilarity of the night of carousing, as well as its very real consequences. The doctors meet for an evening of food and drink and making merry. During the course of the evening, all reason and control disappeared from these otherwise upstanding, well educated, and well-heeled men. There was no plan for this. The well-trained minds of the surgeons could not exert any power to control their actions once their fine-tuned brains were hijacked by alcohol. The consequences that followed this hijacking made once orderly, respectable lives unmanageable. The doctors find themselves in prison, where they spend the rest of their days. They could not admit being powerless. They were unable to surrender, and therefore, unable to recover.

~

Exploring the Powerlessness and Unmanageability of The First Step

1.   Respond to the chapter illustration. What thoughts and feelings does the picture evoke?

2.   Draw "powerlessness." (Remind the participants that the quality of the artwork is irrelevant.)

3.   Talk about the phrase, "cutting off your nose to spite your face." What does it mean to group members? How did each doctor do it? List other cautionary sayings, proverbs, or idioms thrown around by parents, teachers, etc. that are too often ignored. (It's easier to catch flies with honey than it is with vinegar. Be careful what you pray for, you might get it. It's not what you say, it's how you say it. Bite your tongue. No use crying over spilled milk.) Participants can cite examples from their own lives, or the lives of others (celebrities, family members, peers and colleagues) and discuss the advice and its relevance to them.

4.   "Do you relate to these doctors? What do you have in

common with them?" Beginning a discussion with these questions allows participants to talk about the feelings and attitudes that occur under the influence, the degree to which they have experienced them, and the resulting consequences.

5. "What have you lost due to alcohol or drugs?" This listing can be compiled on a board or flip chart to examine the severity of the consequences of continued use of alcohol and drugs. After listing the consequences they and others have suffered, ask the questions, "How much pain is enough? What does it take for someone to stop using?"

～

For the Storyteller

"The Three Army Surgeons" is one of the Grimm Brothers collected tales, but is also found in other cultures. It is AT tale type 660. I first heard this story in 1998 at the National Storytelling Festival in Jonesborough, TN, when Batt Burns took the stage. I have updated the details of the story to appeal to a contemporary audience.

～

Synopsis of the story

When three army surgeons stopped at an inn for the evening, the Landlord asked them about their skills. The first surgeon said he could remove his hand and replace it. The second said that he could remove his eye and replace it, and the third said he could remove his own heart and replace it. No one knew they had a salve that could heal all wounds. Each surgeon made good on his assertion. The hand, the eye, and the heart were removed and given to the kitchen maid to hold until the next day. Although the maid put the body parts into the cupboard, she failed to latch it. So, the barn cat feasted on the body parts. The maid was terrified, so her sweetheart promised to help. He cut off the hand of the thief hanging from the gallows. He cut out the eye of the barn cat. He retrieved the heart from the freshly butchered pig. These were the body parts presented to the surgeons, who reattached them and used the salve. It wasn't long before the surgeon with the pig's heart started to run about like a swine. The surgeon with the cat's eye chased mice, and the surgeon with the thief's hand grabbed money off tables when he passed by. When they realized they had not gotten their own body parts back at the inn, they confronted the landlord who went to find the maid—who was gone. The surgeons threatened the landlord who paid them off. But no amount of money could buy them their own hand, heart or eye.

~

Optional Stories

Icarus and Dadelus. Greek Mythology
    www.primarytexts.co.uk/free_resources/Myths17-21.pdf
"Father Grumbler." France. Lang, A. (1966). *The Brown Fairy Book.*
    New York, NY: McGraw-Hill.
"The Red Shoes." Denmark. Andersen, H. C., Hersholt, J., &

Kredel, F. (1949). *The Complete Andersen: all of the 168 stories by Hans Christian Anderson* New York: Heritage Press.

"The Woman Who Wasn't Herself Anymore." France. Bjurstrom, C. G. (Ed.). (1989). *French Folktales.* NY, NY: Pantheon Books.

"Why the Sea is Salt." Dasent, G. W. (2001). *Popular Tales from Norse Mythology.* Mineola, NY: Dover Publications.

Note: An online search will often lead to a printed text of the above stories.

 **NOTES**

∼ NOTES ∼

THE SECOND STEP

*Came to believe that a power greater than ourselves
could restore us to sanity.*

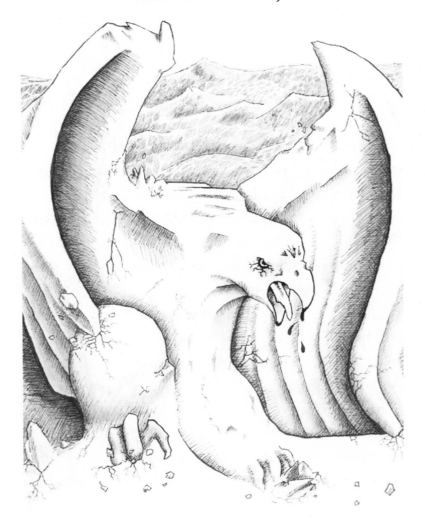

LIKE THE FIRST STEP, THE SECOND STEP has two equally important parts. The first part has to do with finding some level of faith in something other than one's own ego or determination. The second part of the step requires an honest look at one's actions to see the insanity of that behavior, understanding that the behavior is not necessarily clinically or criminally insane. What does insanity look like when it's not a clinical or criminal issue?

THE LEGEND OF DEIDRE:
A TALE TOO SAD FOR THE TELLING
A Celtic Legend

A long time ago, in a small hut on the edge of King Connacher's lands, Deidre and Levarcham watched the snow fall. It was Deidre who broke the silence. "You have always told me stories about great love, great adventure, and great hardship. Stories about feasts and battles, weddings and wooing. But I have never seen anyone save you and the gentle deer that roam the orchard. Where are all these people?"

Levarcham stroked the hair of her foster daughter. It had been fifteen years since King Connacher had charged her with raising Deidre. Their time together had passed slowly and gently, except for the nights when Deirdre would wake from her sleep with a piercing cry.

Visions of a tall man with the mark of the Druid upon his brow haunted her. He invaded her sleep, pointed his finger at her, and warned her of the sorrows she would bear should she leave her seclusion.

Deidre continued, "Will I ever have the life that you told me about? Will I have the courage to face suffering and death? Will I ever know the love of a good man? Bear his children? Is this not my right? Is there a life worth living that is not lived in the challenge of such things?"

Levarcham sensed that Deirdre was becoming a woman, and was having a woman's longings. The wind began to howl as it churned the falling snow into a blizzard. A hunter, lost in the snow, cried out, piercing the silence. "What is that?" cried Deidre. The hunter had seen the smoke from the fire, and was begging to be let in for warmth.

That cry took Levarcham back to King Connacher's Great Hall at Samhain, fifteen years before. It was the same cry that had pierced the merriment of more than a thousand people. As the crowd was hushed, Cathbad, the Druid, approached Malcolm, the King's harper and his wife Elva, who was with child. He pointed at Elva's womb. "That cry has come from the child within.

Her name will be Deidre, and she will be a child of great beauty. From her beauty will arise a sharp sword to split the House of Ulster. It will divide itself, and there will be warfare because of her."

"Kill the child!" The crowd quickly became a mob. King Connacher stood above his subjects like a god, and raised his arms, offering assurance that all was well. But he was intrigued by this prophecy. He would love to have such a powerful beauty at his side. It would enhance his stature. To defeat the prophecy would make him too great a force to be challenged. He would intercede. "It is not good for Elva to see her child die before it is born. This child will be born, and I will have her raised in seclusion. I will marry her myself when she is grown. As my charge, and then as my wife, she will be unable to cause harm. In this way, will I defeat the prophecy." The memory of this moment was so vivid that Levarcham forgot where she was.

"Levarcham!" Deirdre's sharp rebuke pierced Levarcham's rememberings. "I can bear these cries no longer."

"It is only a bird."

"And you taught me that compassion and kindness are important about all else. Even a bird who cries out deserves that as one of God's creatures. If you will not allow this bird to be let in, then I do not think much of your lessons or your faith." And she opened the door.

Deirdre tended to the weary hunter, set him by the hearth, and gave him food and drink. Levarcham cautioned the hunter to keep restraint on his tongue. The hunter didn't hear, for he was enchanted by the beauty of Deidre. A simple gesture from the lass held grace and poetry. He became enchanted. Levarcham's heart filled with fear and foreboding, and her fears were well founded, for once the hunter recovered, he went straight to King Connacher. "I have been rescued and healed by the most beautiful maiden on this earth. I would have been content to sit at her feet and simply gaze at her all the days of my life." The King knew it was time to marry Deidre in order to defeat the prophecy.

King Connacher himself went to that little cottage and told Deidre that they would be wed at the new moon. Deidre became despondent and refused to eat. The King was not the man of her dreams. When Levarcham saw Deidre's distress, she said, "Marrying the King will be the honor of your life!" Deidre gave into despair.

Just before the new moon, Deidre stepped outside the hut to gather firewood. A congress of ravens descended and began to peck at the apples that had fallen in the snow. "That bird is like the man of my dreams. His hair was dark, like the raven's; his skin white like the snow, and his cheeks as red as that apple. That is the man I shall marry." She inhaled deeply, and let out a sigh of great longing. She heard a song floating through the air. Three hunters were upon a path along the edge of the Royal Forest, singing. They took no notice of Deidre. "That is the man of my vision." She dropped the firewood, gathered her skirts, and ran like the wind, compelled by a force she had never known. Her heart throbbed in her chest as she threw herself into his arms. "I saw you in a vision. I will love you forever. At the new moon, they will take me to the King's palace to be his wife. Please! Take me with you!" The hunter peered into her eyes. "My name is Deidre."

The young man trembled, for he realized whom he now held in his arms. "I am Naois, the eldest of the sons of Uisnach, knight of the Red Branch." "Do you not know the prophecy? You have to marry the King. There is still time for you to return." Deidre knew not of the prophecy. "If it is my fate to marry King Connacher, then why do you come to me in my dreams? I saw you before I ever saw you, and loved you before I ever loved you." She dissolved into sobs.

"I saw you before I saw you, and loved you before I ever loved you. But for my honor, I cannot steal what belongs to the king." He turned and ran towards his brothers, but was stopped by a woman's cry of desperation. He turned to see Deidre running to him. She flung herself into his arms and kissed him.

"I value this moment more than ten lifetimes with Connacher." Deidre looked through Naois 'eyes and deep into his soul. Then and there, they pledged their love. When they caught up with Allen and Arden, the brothers welcomed their new sister. Knowing the prophecy and the danger they invited, they went into exile, to Alba, which is Scotland. The brothers built a home at the top of a waterfall. Their life was rich and full and hard, just like the stories Levarcham had told Deidre. They were content and happy. Time moved slowly and beautifully.

During that time, King Connacher made peace with those he had not destroyed. His kingdom prospered, and the King became restless. He went to see Cathbad, the druid. "Our warriors, Naois, Allen and Arden, are not amongst us. It is not fitting that they should be in exile because of a mere woman. I will send Fergus Mac Roigh to Alba to announce a king's pardon and invite them to a great feast, here, at Emhain Macha. Cathbad was silent.

Fergus arrived in Alba three days later with the king's message. Naois, Allen, and Arden welcomed their kinsman, and were starving for news from home. The stories about the victories of King Connacher lasted far into the night. When Naois finally crept into bed and wrapped his arms around Deidre, he shared his longing for home and told her the good news. Deidre was horrified. "No, my love. It is a trap. I had a dream of three hawks flying in from the south with honey in their beaks, and they took away three drops of blood. The three drops of blood are Allen and Arden, and you, my soul." Naois pushed Deidre and the warning aside. "Connacher vowed forgiveness and longs to have the strong arm of us, his foster brothers, at his side again. Fergus is a man of honor, and my kinsman. I trust him. We sail tomorrow." Deidre cried and hardly slept.

The four of them left the shores of Alba at dawn. As they sailed into the night, Deidre picked up her harp and sang haunting songs of betrayal. By dawn, the shores of Ireland were in plain sight, and they traveled easily to Emain Macha. Word was sent that the sons of Uisnach were ready to meet their king.

But the King was not ready to receive them. "Take them to the Inn of the Red Branch for the night. I will receive them tomorrow." Later that night, Connacher summoned one hundred warriors to his great hall." Go to the Inn and kill the sons of Uisnach, and bring Deidre to me." The brothers fought with such noble hearts that each was equal to twenty warriors. The grass became a slippery pool of blood, and when it was done, the brothers defeated all hundred men.

The sons of Uisnach realized they would be forever exiled to Alba, and began racing towards the shore with Deidre. Connacher summoned Cathbad, the Druid. "Stop them!" Cathbad raised a forest on the great plain, but the brothers went through it easily. "Stop them!!" raged the King. The druid changed the plain into a freezing sea. Deidre climbed upon Naois' shoulder, and they swam against the current and continued to make progress. Before Connacher could threaten the druid, Cathbad turned the sea into sharp, moving stones, like swords posed upwards. The brothers ran upon the stones, slipped and fell many times. Allen cried out as he fell and perished. Naois looked for Arden, but saw Arden disappear between the stones. The will to live was torn from Naois. Not even Deidre could sustain him. Naois slipped upon the rocks, and died without a word. "It is done," whispered the Druid.

"Good. Now dry up the flood," ordered Connacher. Cathbad raised his arms one last time, to leave the sons of Uisnach dead on the green plain. Deidre cradled Naois. "My beloved, I can no longer eat or smile. Soon enough I shall lie in my grave." Connacher ordered her taken away and locked in his palace.

Naois, Allen, and Arden were buried where they lay, and that place was marked with a stone. The prophecy of Deidre had come true. Many men died because of her, and the Red Branch had been divided. Although Deidre stayed in Connacher's household, he took no pleasure in her. She neither ate, nor slept, and on the morning of her wedding, she was dead. King Connacher ordered Deidre buried at the cottage where she had lived with Levarcham, but a band of people moved the grave to the great plain, near the grave of Naois. Each grave was especially marked with a stake of Yew. Almost instantly, the stakes of wood sprouted tiny leaves and began to grow towards each other, reaching out with their branches until they could touch. The branches intertwined so that the two trees were one. All of this happened a long time ago, but the trees still stand to this day.

~

Discussion of "Deidre of the Sorrows"
As it relates to the Second Step

There is much written about the alcoholic's desire to "play God" (AA Basic Text, 2006, p.62). King Conchubar presents himself as just that—the one who can defeat the gods and their prophecy and refuses to see himself as powerless or as having any measure of unmanageability in his life or his kingdom. Yet, the insanity of Conchubar's actions is glaringly evident. A once-prosperous and harmonious existence has been destroyed because one man was determined to "play God." It must be said that the King believes he is acting in the best interests of his kingdom, yet this appearance of benevolence is simply a mask to hide his selfish and corrupt motives. And so it is with the addict in active addiction, pursuing the drug of choice no matter what (Naaken, 1996).

Deidre is the other character who illustrates this "self will run riot" that is described in the AA's Basic Text (2006). For Deidre, Naoise has become the drug of choice, as Deidre has become his. Naoise is well aware of the consequences of defying his King by stealing the King's betrothed. Deidre is not. She is in a blissful state of denial, refusing to see the unmanageability of her life and the insanity of her actions.

The entire kingdom suffers, much as the entire family suffers when there is an active alcoholic or addict in the family. In the family of the alcoholic/addict, family members assume the roles of the enabler, the scapegoat, the orphan, and the mascot; each manifesting the addiction in their own way (Woitiz, 1983). The characters in this story assume those same roles. Both the King and Deidre can be compared to the addict/alcoholic. The Druid and Levercham, the storyteller, are both enablers, promoting the King's destructive desires by being "dutiful servants." Naoise becomes the Scapegoat, as he is the victim of both Deidre and the King, and the identified problem. The brothers, Allan and Arden, assume the Orphan roles in this family, invisible, having no voice, going along with whatever force is present.

It is important to consider how life might have unfolded for Deidre and Naoise had they not returned home. Had they stayed away, the young lovers would have at least been safe.

Returning home was their demise. People new to recovery are advised and encouraged to change people, places, and things in order to recover from active addiction, but separating from family can be difficult, if not impossible. The story of Deidre not only illustrates the first two Steps. It can also be seen as a cautionary tale about family disease of addiction,

∼

Exploring the Misuse of Power and the Insanity of The Second Step

1.   Before sharing the story ask, "What does this illustration tell you about the story?"

2.   Draw the part of the story that spoke to you. Share the

picture with the group and share how you related to that moment in the story.

3.   Is there a character with whom you relate? What are the similarities between you and that character?

4.   Although Deidre had her needs for food, clothing, and shelter met, she was not content. What was missing in her life? Can you identify with that discontent?

5.   Put the characters of the story into the roles that exist in an alcoholic/addicted family.

Who is the addict/alcoholic? The enabler? The mascot? The lost child? The scapegoat? The hero? What role did denial play in this situation? What truth-telling needed to happen to avoid disaster?

6.   Examine the spirituality in the story. The Druids were the spiritual leaders of the Celtic world and were the king's advisors. Describe and discuss the role that the gods and the Druid played in the story. What happened when the King tried to "play God?" How does that compare to the modern relationship between a person and their pastor? Does faith require a formal practice or structure?

7.   Insanity has been described as "Doing the same thing and expecting different results." Is there evidence of that kind of thinking in the story? Can you relate to that definition of insanity?

~

For the Storyteller

This Celtic Legend is found in many collections of Celtic or Irish myths and legends. My adaptation is based on the version found in *Myths and Folklore of Ireland* compiled by Jeremiah Curtain and was originally published in 1890.

~

Synopsis of the Story

A prophecy is delivered that a child yet unborn will destroy the kingdom. To avoid panic and the murder of the pregnant mother, the King declares that the child will be raised in secret and he will marry her himself to defeat the prophecy. The child, Deidre, is raised in secret by the King's storyteller. When Deidre comes of age, she is anxious to come out of hiding and experience the world. That is when her caretaker tells Deidre she will marry the King. Deidre wants none of that. She wants to experience life and love as she has in her dreams. By chance, she sees Naoise and his brothers in the forest, instantly falls in love, and convinces the three of them to take her away. They go to Scotland, happy but homesick. They cannot return home because they have stolen the King's bride. Furious that his bride has been stolen, the King manipulates the group to return home. When they arrive, they are met with natural and unnatural destructive forces. The brothers are killed, left to rot in the fields, and Deirdre is taken to the palace. The townsfolk bury the brothers where they lay. When the King sends for Deidre on their wedding day, Deidre is found dead. She is buried next to her beloved, and the yew branches that marked their graves grew together into one tree.

Optional Stories

"The Man Who Wanted to Be Snakebit" Erdoes, R. (1998). *Legends and tales of the American West*. New York: Pantheon Books.

"If God is Everywhere." Abrahams, R. D. (Ed.). (1983). *African Folktales: Traditional Stories of the Black World*. NY: Pantheon Books.

"Walking on Water" Abrahams, R. D. (Ed.). (1983). *African Folktales: Traditional Stories of the Black World*. NY: Pantheon Books.

"Snake's Jive" http://healingstory.org/ Allison Cox

"The Magic Ball" http://healingstory.org/ Joan Stockbridge

"Pandora's Box" www.greekmyths-greekmythology.com/pandoras-box-myth/

Note: An online search will often lead to a printed text of the above stories.

∼ NOTES ∼

∼ NOTES ∼

THE THIRD STEP

*Made a decision to turn our will and our lives over
to the care of God as we understood him.*

THE THIRD STEP CAN BE ACCOMPLISHED in the blink of an eye. All one has to do is make a decision. No physical action is required. How we see God or what name we call a supreme being is irrelevant. What is required is a willingness to admit that we have not been terribly successful in managing our own lives and that new management is desperately needed.

Three frogs are sitting on a log. Two frogs decide to jump. How many frogs are left?

THE HANDLESS MAIDEN
Adapted from the Brothers Grimm

Dressed as an old man, the devil approached a poor Miller and told the man that his fortunes could change if he would grant the Devil what grew behind the mill. The Miller thought for a moment. The only thing behind the mill was an old apple tree that no longer bore fruit, so he agreed. Suddenly, the miller's wife came storming out of the house.

"What have you done? I opened the cupboard, and jewels spilled out, falling onto the ground. I opened the pie safe and found gold coins in crocks lining the pie safe. What have you done?" When the Miller told his wife how good fortune came to them, she began shrieking.

"You fool! Your daughter was pruning the tree behind the mill! You sold your daughter! Your only child! How could you!" The Miller was sickened by what he had done, but he knew he had no choice but to keep the bargain. Being a dutiful child, the daughter knew she had no choice but to serve the old man (the

Devil).

The night before she was to be taken, she washed herself so clean that her skin glowed. She dressed in white and drew a protective circle around herself. When the old man reached for her, he was repelled by the goodness and purity that protected her. She could not be touched.

"I'll have my prize! Take this disobedient child and tie her to the apple tree so that she cannot bathe before I return. You will keep your bargain." Tears streamed down the miller's cheeks as he tied his only child to the apple tree. As the dutiful daughter, she followed his lead. That night, torrential rains came down, soaking the girl's clothes and hair. Mud splashed into her face and eyes and hair. When the rain subsided, the poor wretched child began to cry. She cried so hard and so long that she cried herself clean, and again her skin glowed. Her dress was as white as it was when she first put it on. Again, the old man could not touch the goodness and purity that radiated from this girl.

"AAUUGHH! You have tricked me for the last time, sir. You let her bathe. I know it. You did! But now, you will cut off her hands so that she cannot bathe!" The Miller knew that if he did not do this horrible thing, they would all die.

"Father, do what you must. I am your child. I will obey." She bared her wrists for her father. He cut her hands off. And once more, his daughter cried so loud and so long that she cried herself clean. The stumps scabbed over. Once more, the devil could not touch her and left in disgust.

The Miller approached his only child. "Please forgive me. I

will love you and care for you the rest of your life. Please. I love you."

"No. If I stay with you, I will become like you. I need to go." She left, and wandered until she was exhausted and starving. She saw an orchard inside the moat that protected the King's castle. She closed her eyes and asked to be fed. An angel swept her up and away and over the water. After the girl had regained her bearings and her balance, she walked towards the fruit trees that seemed to bend towards her and to touch her mouth. While she ate pears in the orchard, the royal gardener brought the girl to the King's attention. The King took the wounded girl in. He ordered silver hands be made for her. She was grateful to him, and after a time, the two fell in love and were wed. Their bliss was cut short. War had come to the kingdom.

While the King was away in battle, a baby was born. The Queen Mother sent word to her son that the heir to the throne had been born and that mother and son were both in good health.

The Devil, who had been biding his time, intercepted the message. The message that the old man delivered said, "Son, your wife has delivered a changeling. His mother must be a witch. What would you have me do?" The King's response was to care for his wife and his son until his return, that it didn't matter to him if the child was a changeling or not.

What the Queen Mother received, however, was a message to kill the Queen and the baby. She could not and did not, but she did advise the young Queen and the baby to flee the castle, and take refuge with a wise woman who lived in the woods nearby.

Deep in the forest, a crone took them in and loved them instantly. She gave the Queen healing teas and poultices for her stumps. The Queen cradled her son with her silver hands and cried. She took him to a pond to bathe him and to bathe her stumps, and she cried. She asked for grace, and she cried. One day, when she was bathing her son, he slipped from her arms.

Panic-stricken, the Queen plunged her stumps into the water to find him and was able to catch him in her hands that had been restored. She was whole once more.

When the King arrived home and learned the truth, he went in search of his family. He promised to not rest in the same place two nights in a row until he found them. Seven years later, the boy-child found him, looking like a poor wanderer in the forest who needed food and shelter. The boy brought the wanderer to the cottage. The King stared at the child's mother. She knew instantly who he was. He finally spoke.

"Forgive me, but don't I know you? There is something familiar and wonderful about you.

You remind me of my wife, but my wife had silver hands, and you do not."

"But I do." She produced the silver hands, now tarnished. After the identity of all was revealed and the story had been pieced together, the royal family returned their kingdom united, to rule with justice, fairness, and compassion all the rest of their days.

～

Discussion of "The Handless Maiden"
As It Applies to the Third Step

Three frogs are sitting on a log. Two frogs decide to jump. How many frogs are left? The answer is three. A decision is made in the mind. No overt, obvious, or physical action required. This is nothing more than the realization that we have been unsuccessful in managing our lives and the consequences of our actions, and that we need help. In a civilized society, when someone cannot manage his own life, someone else takes over.

Our society has given the legal system and the department of social services the task of managing lives that are out of control. In all fairness, there are those who, because of physical or mental limitations, need the support of the established systems. Once the alcoholic/addict loses control of his life, his actions bring him to the attention of those same systems. The arrests for drunk driving, the neglect or abuse of a child, stealing, domestic violence, and distribution of controlled substances are the actions of addicts and alcoholics. This third step simply asks the recovering person to recognize the folly of their actions, to ask for help, and then follow those suggestions. For the purposes of this step, and to avoid religious debate, let's treat the word "God" as an acronym for "Good Orderly Direction."

Children are often the victims of a parent's addiction. To bring a child into the world and not fulfill the parental role is the worst sort of betrayal. These children are neglected, lacking the basic necessities of life, or abused physically or sexually. They are often without a voice, a choice, or an advocate, and the experience has been classified as a trauma. As trauma survivors, these children are susceptible to a multitude of mental health disorders. "The Handless Maiden" is a story of parental betrayal and abuse. A daughter is betrayed by her parents and becomes incapable of the activities of daily living. Once maimed, the heroine embodies the powerlessness of The First Step. But she doesn't give up or give in to despair. As the heroine embarks on her path of recovery, she trusts implicitly that she will survive, despite the handicap of losing her hands. And she does.

A magical helper appears and helps the heroine overcome the barriers to the fruit in the King's orchard. Some Divine force, some Higher Power, has made itself known, and has helped without expecting payment. Here, the heroine must rely on faith and trust, which is a new construct for the newly recovering person. The Second and Third Steps of Alcoholics Anonymous suggest that a Higher Power of one's own choosing will intervene, and will care about each person who takes those steps in earnest, expecting nothing in return. A newcomer's ability to successfully leave home, or the addictive lifestyle, often depends upon some belief system that will sustain her in difficult times and circumstances. That decision is the essence of The Third Step.

It is easy to expect that life will be wonderful and without heartbreak if one can manage to stay sober. However, life continues to happen to all of us, sober or not. People divorce, people die, people lose their livelihood, deal with natural disasters, sober or not. Staying sober and keeping the faith are challenging when the bottom falls out of a life that has been re-built in sobriety. Once safe, and married to the King, the handless maiden had every right to believe that she would live "happily ever after." But she doesn't.

The heroine finds herself forsaken by someone she loves, and hits a second "bottom" in this story. Refusing to give up, she enters the wood, the archetypal sanctuary, and is taken in by the wise woman, the healer, the crone who lives there. The heroine's miracle of healing came as a result of her willingness to trust that she would survive the journey, her willingness to cry until there were no more tears, her willingness to change. This belief in a benevolent universe that will sustain her is as viable a belief system as any organized religion. The story can open a conversation about belief systems and spirituality as a basis for living, much as the Twelve Steps suggest a spiritual basis for living.

~

Exploring questions of trust, faith, and belief required for The Third Step

1. Bob for apples. Consider what it would take to survive if this were your only means of finding and eating food.

2. React/respond to the illustration. What moment would you have chosen to best illustrate the story? Drawing that moment is also an option.

3. Consider the other options the family of origin had. Did the Miller (the father) have any other viable options?

Where was the mother? Why didn't she put a stop to this? Why was it okay to sacrifice the daughter?

4.   What other options did the Queen Mother have when told to kill her daughter-in-law and her grandson? Why didn't she sacrifice them?

5.   How is the devil in the story like the disease of addiction?

6.   The maiden cries herself clean, and then cries herself whole. How do you feel about crying? What were you taught/told about crying in your family of origin? (List them on a flip chart or a whiteboard.) Share the personal stories that go with those sayings. What behaviors did you adopt as a result? How well do those rules serve you now?

7.   Explore the difference between being a victim, playing the victim, and taking personal responsibility for one's life. In which category is the maiden? Her father? Her mother? The Prince?

8.   "Bloom where you are planted." "When life gives you lemons, make lemonade." The heroine does just that. How does she do that? How could you do that?

9.   The Maiden sets out on her journey with a blind faith that she will survive. When does she make that decision? Who/what is that power in which she believes? What is faith? Is it different than religion? Different than spirituality?

~

For the Storyteller

Many cultures have a version of this tale. This version was chosen because it addresses the abuse that many addicted women have endured. I first heard Susan Gordon tell her version of the Grimms' story during a storytelling class in her barn in Ijamsville, MD. Her version is contained in *Feminist Messages: Coding in Women's Folk Culture*, Joan Newlon Radner, editor, University of Illinois, Chicago, 1993. My adaptation draws from both Gordon's rendition and the Grimm Brothers version. It is AT tale type 706 with versions of this story in many cultures, including Xhosa, South Africa, Germany, France, Spain, Russia, and Japan.

~

Synopsis of the story

A poor miller is approached by the devil and is given the promise of riches beyond his wildest dreams in exchange for what is behind the barn. The Miller agrees, not realizing his daughter is behind the barn. The daughter says she will obey her father. When it is time for the devil to come for the maiden, she dresses in white and draws a chalk circle around her body. The devil cannot cross the line. Furious, the devil demands that the maid be tied to a tree so that she will be filthy when he returns for her. She cries herself clean, and once again, the devil cannot take her. The Devil demands that the Miller cut off the maiden's hands, so she cannot clean herself. The Miller does just that, but once again, the maiden cries herself so clean the Devil cannot touch her. He leaves in disgust.

Despite the words of love, and offers of support, the maiden leaves her home. She wanders until she comes upon a moat. Just beyond the moat is an orchard that surrounds the King's castle. An ethereal being picks up the maiden and takes her to the orchard. The trees bend down to her so she can eat. The gardener reports this to the King, who then witnesses this phenomenon. He approached her and offers her sanctuary. She accepts, and after a time, they fall in love and marry. The King has silver hands fashioned for her as a gift. In time, she becomes pregnant. Then, the King gets word that he must go to war. He leaves his bride in the care of his mother.

In the King's absence, a child is born. The Queen mother sends word to her son, but the message is intercepted by the Devil. What the King receives is the message that his son is a changeling. The King responds to keep his bride and his son safe. The message that the Queen Mother receives is to kill the Queen and the son and to keep their hearts as proof. The Queen Mother sends her daughter-in-law and her grandson into the woods, to an old crone who takes them in. While living with the crone, the maiden's hands grow back.

When the King returns from war and finds his family gone, he goes in search of them.

He searches for seven years. One day, he naps in a field and is awakened by a seven-year-old boy, who takes him home. The King sees the resemblance to his wife, but says, "my wife had silver hands." The heroine produces the silver hands, and the family is reunited.

∿

Optional Stories

"The Stone Cutter" Japan. Lang, A. (1947). *Crimson Fairy Book.*
Collected and edited by A. Lang. Illustrated by Ben Kutcher,
etc. New York :Longmans, Green & Co.

"The Girl Who was Poor and Good" Greece. Ragan, K. (1998).
Fearless Girls, Wise Women & Beloved Sisters. New York:
W.W. Norton.

"What Happens When You Really Believe" Africa. Abrahams, R.
D. (Ed.). (1983). *African Folktales: Traditional Stories of the
Black World.* NY: Pantheon Books.

"King Solomon's Quest" Traditional Jewish. Stone, S. (2009).
Storytelling Magazine, 21(3), 7.

"Tam Lin" Scotland. Barchers, S. I., & Mullineaux, L. (1990).
Wise Women: Folk and Fairy Tales from Around the World.
Libraries Unlimited Incorporated.

Note: an online search will often lead to a printed text of these stories.

∿ **NOTES** ∿

∿ NOTES ∿

THE FOURTH STEP

Made a searching and fearless inventory of ourselves

"YOU WANT ME TO DO WHAT?!" The newcomer protests, procrastinates, and avoids the task of writing down all that stuff they did during active addiction.

"The same person will drink or use again," is the collective wisdom of the Twelve Step Fellowship, and until we know who and what we are, we cannot change. Thinking about the Fourth Step is far worse than just doing it. Just as the recovery journey starts with the first step, this inventory starts with the first word. On the other side of this work is the freedom to never have to look over your shoulder again.

BUNDLES OF TROUBLES
A German folktale

A woman was riding through the desert, alone, weighed down with her provisions, her troubles, and her own thoughts. The desert sun blistered her skin and scorched her throat.

Weary down to her bones, the woman plodded through the Wasteland, determined to make it through. She saw someone in the distance, a Crone, an old woman, who beckoned her.

"Come inside where it is cool and dark. Lay down your bundle of troubles and rest. I will tether your horse and tend to him while you sleep." Sleep came easily, and the traveler's dreams were sweet. The woman slept until she was rested. When she awoke, she took stock of her surroundings. There were mounds of saddlebags and satchels in the cave, staring back at her as though they had eyes. The Crone appeared with a glass of cucumber water. While the traveler gulped the refreshing liquid, the Crone spoke.

"Many a soul has come to rest here, laying down their bundles of troubles. Each person who comes here has the chance to exchange their bundle of troubles for a new one. It's your turn now. You came with a bundle, and you will leave with one. It doesn't have to be the one that you had when you came inside. Choose any bundle. The only stipulation is that you may not look inside."

A pair of weary and desperate eyes scanned the mounds of saddlebags and satchels. The traveler picked up many of them, testing the weight, poking the contents, and shaking it to see if the troubles rattled inside. She was drawn to the saddlebags that were jeweled, but their weight was too much for her tiny frame. There was one with tooled leather, painted with beautiful flowers and butterflies. When she picked it up, the dye from the flowers stained her hands and made them itch and burn. Finally, she settled on a sturdy, well-made set of saddlebags and thanked the Crone for giving her respite. Once outside in the harsh desert sun, she realized the bags were her very own. They didn't feel quite so heavy anymore. She pushed herself and her steed through the desert sands, taking a mental inventory of her troubles.

There were the lies she had told, the promises she had broken, the duties she failed to fulfill. There were the missed appointments and botched opportunities, financial burdens created and compounded by actions taken or actions postponed. There were the unresolved arguments, broken relationships, and dreams deferred. This listing of troubles brought her to tears.

Just before the sun dipped below the horizon, she found a place to tether her horse and build a fire. Using her saddlebags as a pillow, and the horse's blanket for warmth, she slept. In her dream, a voice spoke with great authority. "Woman, go down to the river and fill your saddlebags with rocks. In the morning, you will be both happy and sad." Her dream self dragged herself out of that deep sleep and listened for the sound of rushing water. She followed that sound until she was standing ankle deep in running water. She knelt and began putting river rocks in the sturdy leather bags. Fearing that the leather would give under the weight of too many rocks, she stopped when the bags were only half full. "This is good enough." When the morning sun awoke her dream self, she emptied the saddlebags. It wasn't rocks that tumbled out, it was jewels. She realized she was, indeed, both happy and sad.

She awoke with a gasp. It was really a dream, wasn't it? Just in case, she reached for her saddlebags and peered inside. All of her troubles were still there, but so were the good parts. Her courage, her compassion, her sense of humor, the way she cared for her children and her aging parents. Her beautiful singing voice that brought tears to the eyes of others, and her resilience in the face of tragedy or crisis. She took a deep breath, embraced who she was, and let go of the pain.

～

Discussion of "Bundles of Troubles" As It Relates to the Fourth Step

This woman carries the burdens of life so heavily that she needed to find relief. The saddlebags she carries symbolize this burden that can, and will, feed an addiction. The Crone, having seen this despair before, takes the burden for awhile so that the woman can rest. When given the choice of all the other burdens in the cave, the woman picks up her own bundle, feeling differently about its weight. When she finally looks inside, she can see the totality of her life.

Any business taking an inventory will identify both assets and liabilities. This step should be no different. While it is important to take stock of the damage done in active addiction, it is also important to see that "there is a bit of bad in the best of us, and a bit of good in the worst of us." Recognizing that who we are is the sum total of all our experiences is one of the gifts of The Fourth Step. The bundles she carries make our heroine the woman she is.

Many come into recovery with no self-concept, self-esteem, or self-knowledge. Many are driven by guilt, shame, and/or remorse. Many have survived some level of trauma and believed that it was the result of their own actions, or that it was deserved. The process of taking a long hard look at oneself allows us to see to what extent we are responsible, and to what extent we participated knowingly and willingly. Who we become as sober people is the combination of all we have experienced. Self-acceptance and serenity come from the recognition of who we are, and who we are not. Completing the fourth step is the first action step in that process. Steps Five through Nine take us the rest of the way.

∼

Exploring the fear of self-appraisal needed in The Fourth Step

1. Draw your "saddlebags" on a large piece of drawing paper. Identify your strengths, and record them on one color of sticky notes, one strength per note. Put them onto the drawing. Using another color of sticky notes, identify your liabilities, and write one per sticky note. Attach them onto the drawing. Pair each liability with a strength that will allow you to work to correct/change the situation. Strengths may need to be used more than once. Talk about the experience of seeing your strengths and liabilities on paper.

2. Provide a variety of magazines, supplies for making a collage, and two brown paper bags, one large, one small. Cut out images and words that show how we present ourselves to the world, and glue them to the large bag. Cut out images and words that reveal the hidden parts of us, and glue them to the smaller bag. If there is time, have other participants cut out words and images that illustrated how the others in the group see the individual, and have the other group members place them inside the bag as a gift.

3. Draw a treasure map of your life by identifying 3-6 major events from your past.

4.   The illustration shows two women of different generations. What do their facial expressions reveal about their state of mind and their relationship?

5.   Dreams are said to be the subconscious mind at work. The young woman's dream contains a paradox, that rocks are really jewels. How is that possible?

⌒

For the Storyteller

Allison Cox's adaptation of "Bundles of Troubles, Bundles of Blessings" was the basis for my re-telling of this German folktale. Allison's version is posted on the Healing Story Alliance website. http://healingstory.org/ She cites *A Piece Of The Wind*, by Ruthilde Kronberg and Patricia McKissack, Harper, San Francisco, 1990 as her source. I incorporated the traditional tale, "Half Full" into my version, which was recorded by Meliss Bunce.

⌒

Synopsis

A woman is crossing the desert on horseback, burdened with heavy saddlebags. She sees a cave in the distance, with an old woman standing at the mouth of the cave. The old woman beckons to her. The younger woman dismounts and walks into the cave. An old woman, the Crone, takes the reins from the traveler and tells her to lay down her saddlebags and rest.

When the young woman has rested, the crone tells her she

needn't take her own bundle of troubles, but that she may have any bundle she wants. After testing many for weight and sturdiness, she leaves with her own bundle. By the time she stops to make camp for the night, she is again feeling burdened.

She has a dream that night in which a woman is told to fill her saddlebags with river rock, and that in the morning; she will be both happy and sad. When the woman in the dream fills the bags half full, she gets too tired to finish. The dream continues with the woman awaking and peering into the saddlebags. As predicted, the woman in the dream is both happy and sad, because the saddlebags were now half full of jewels.

The woman wakes and checks her saddlebags to make sure it was a dream. She looked inside, and saw her troubles, but also saw her good qualities, qualities that would see her through it all. She let out a sigh and let go of the pain.

～

Optional Stories

"He Starved His Own" (Africa). Abrahams, R. D. (Ed.). (1983). *African Folktales: Traditional Stories of the Black World.* NY: Pantheon Books.

"Half a Blanket" (Traditional Jewish). Schram, P. (2008). *The Hungry Clothes and Other Jewish Folktales.* NY: Sterling Publishing.

"The Boy who Cried Wolf" (Greece). Jones, V. V. (Trans.). (2003). *Aesop's fables.* NY: Barnes and Noble Classics.

"Truth and Falsehood" (Greece). Yolen, J. (2008). *Favorite folktales from around the world.* New York: Pantheon Books

"Tam Lin" (Ireland). Barchers, S. I., & Mullineaux, L. (1990). *Wise Women: Folk and Fairy Tales from Around the World.* Libraries Unlimited Incorporated.

Note: an online search will often lead to a printed text of these stories.

 **NOTES**

∼ NOTES ∼

THE FIFTH STEP

Admitted to God, to ourselves, and to another human being the exact nature of our wrongs

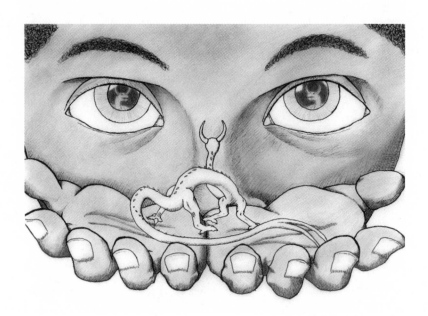

WE ARE TOLD THAT CONFESSION IS GOOD FOR THE SOUL. However, exposing our secrets feels too personal ... too invasive. It's especially threatening to reveal the actions that occurred because we stooped to behaviors that we knew were disgusting and revolting. So why would anyone subject himself to such scrutiny?

THE MONSTER WHO GREW SMALL
A folktale from Ethiopia

Once there was a young lad named Miobe who lived in the jungle, where all sorts of creatures lurked beneath, in the lush brush that was the jungle floor. Most of the boys in the village found the jungle to be a never-ending source of adventure and daring. Any single step could spell disaster and often did, for some poor unwitting soul who didn't look before stepping.

And one only had to look up to see creatures that could climb or leap or fly onto an unsuspecting explorer who had disturbed a nest, or a lair, or a tunnel that some animal called home. That was not the case for Miobe, whose name meant "The Frightened One." Miobe knew that the inside the jungle were untold dangers, just like the quicksand that devoured everything precious and important, including his pet mongoose.

Miobe didn't save his beloved pet from the quicksand. He merely watched in horror as his furry buddy disappeared, too afraid to even try to save him. Miobe just let the mongoose die. Miobe never told the truth about his pet; he simply refused to enter the jungle ever again. That prompted the jeering of the village boys. Their taunts were as painful as the episode with the fire ants or the snake bite that he had, in fact, endured. Those injuries healed. The wounds of the words did not. Miobe could no longer live with the shame of being afraid. He needed to find his strength. He needed to find his backbone. He needed to find his courage.

Miobe began this quest. Just venturing into the jungle and staying through the night was a terrifying challenge, but Miobe only had to confront his own memories and fearful imaginings. By staying several days in the jungle, Miobe had to endure pangs of hunger, and scavenge enough edible bugs to survive. But, mere survival wasn't enough. There had been no enemy, no battle for Miobe to win. Winning was necessary to be considered brave. Miobe wanted to be brave.

He continued his journey through the jungle until he came upon a village that had been leveled by fire. The villagers were huddled in a cave at the edge of the village, terrified to see the light of day, and poised to defend their loved ones and their lives. Miobe approached carefully, not knowing if he would be attacked. With gentle words, Miobe introduced himself to the villagers, who then shared their story. There had been a fire-breathing monster, which had the head of a crocodile, the body of a rhinoceros, and a tail like an elephant's trunk that could hold a man while the head roasted him. While roasting his dinner, the flames from the monster's nostrils ignited everything else in the village…the huts, the stables, the cooking pits, the weaver's looms, as well as, the animals and humans he found distasteful. They had fled for their lives, but had no idea how they would survive with the monster on the hunt.

This was the battle Miobe was craving. This would make Miobe the Brave One! "I'll kill the monster!" declared Miobe, and he began his trek up the mountain. Miobe's heart was pounding so hard it felt as though it would burst. When Miobe stopped to get his breath, he looked up. There was the monster breathing fire! It did have the head of a crocodile, and the body of a rhino. It was a big as the Royal Barge! The trunk-like tail was holding up a tiger that was being roasted! This was too gruesome. Miobe turned and worked his way back down the mountain. When Miobe felt safe once more, he looked over his shoulder at the mountaintop.

Now the monster was the size of five Royal Barges! Five!

Five? How was that possible? How could the monster grow bigger when Miobe was farther away? Miobe sat down on a rock to ponder the question. It didn't make any sense. It wasn't possible. Was it? Miobe knew he needed to confront this monster and prove himself to be brave, no matter how terrified he was. Just then, the monster roared, and sent a burst of flames down the mountain, igniting everything in its path. Miobe took a deep breath, closed his eyes, and ran towards the monster. The heat singed the hair on Miobe's arms and legs. Then, as a cool breeze that swept through the air, Miobe opened his eyes.

Miobe's eyes scanned the landscape for a monster the size of the Royal Barge, with the head of a crocodile, the body of a rhino, and a tail like an elephant's trunk. The monster was nowhere to be found. Something warm brushed across Miobe's foot. He looked down and saw a very small creature the size of a newborn kitten. It had the head of a crocodile, the body of a rhino, and a tail like an elephant's trunk. It tried to be ferocious. Instead, a puff of smoke came out of its nostrils…not fire. Miobe picked it up and stroked its head. Then, the monster began to purr.

Miobe put the tiny creature on his shoulder and came down the mountain whistling. The villagers came running to see this great hero who had destroyed the fire-breathing monster!

Imagine their shock when they saw the baby monster on Miobe's shoulder. So many questions were asked all at once! It was impossible to hear each one, much less answer them. A little girl perched on her father's shoulder leaned over to pet the tiny monster. "What's your name?" she asked.

The monster looked about, to see that everyone was listening. "My name is FEAR."

Some say Miobe attained his full adult height as he walked down that mountain. Others say that while holding Fear in the palm of his hand, Miobe became a man. He had been transformed. However, Miobe will tell you that he simply was no longer ashamed of having been afraid.

～

Discussion of "The Monster Who Grew Small"
As It Relates to the Fifth Step

Miobe's story about facing fear is the experience of virtually every person who works the Fifth Step. The precursor is Step Four, which is taken by one's self, in the safety of home or sanctuary. We write down the resentments, harms, and fears, which is cathartic in and of itself. However, it is not nearly as powerful as sharing that with another human being. Facing that next step, exposing one's secrets and recounting one's wrongs out loud, generates tremendous fear. It doesn't matter that confession is good for the soul. The fear is that WE are the monster who have perpetrated untold misery on the planet, and that there shall be no forgiveness. We are terrified of taking ownership of the past because it makes one responsible for past actions. And yet, exposing the secrets and the fear to the light of day brings relief. We sit with a sponsor, a trusted friend or mentor, or perhaps a priest, and tell the secrets. There is no more need to hide in the shadows. The fear loses its power, just as the monster loses its power in the story. We discover, "We're just not that good at being bad." We experience acceptance for perhaps the first time in our lives.

~

For insights into the fears that keep us isolated, silent, and ashamed

1. Have a discussion about the various acronyms for "fear:"

    False Evidence Appearing Real

    Forget Everything And Run

    Face Everything And Recover

2. Invite each group member to write a secret on an index

card. This may be a real secret or a fabricated one. However, the fabricated one must be plausible. The group facilitator collects the index cards, shuffles them and then passes them out randomly. Each group member takes a turn sharing the secret that was handed to them as though it was their own, and receives feedback from the group. Group members need never disclose their own secret unless they are ready and willing to do so. After the secrets have been shared, group members process what it was like to hear their secret shared and discussed.

3.   Define or describe acts of courage. List them for the group to examine. Further examine the list to identify heroic acts. What qualities does a hero possess? List them.

4.   Describe the person who is always the last one to be picked. What qualities does this person possess? How could the community, the team, the club, the class be more supportive and encouraging? List those ideas. Challenge the group members to adopt one of those strategies to use with someone who is marginalized by the group.

∽

For the Storyteller

"The Monster who Grew Small" has been retold and published by Joan Grant. The notes simply identify it as a folktale from Ethiopia. Other variations can be found on the Searching Out Stories website: http://www.story-lovers.com/listsofstories.html

~

Synopsis of the story

Miobe (The Frightened One) had been branded the coward of the village. Miobe had chosen safety rather than adventure. When he could stand it no more, he decided to leave the village in order to find his courage. He came upon a village that had been leveled by fire. The villagers were all huddled together, terrified to leave their homes to visit, to hunt, to have adventures. Miobe found this curious and asked about the terror that has them so confined.

The villagers told the story of a monster who lived at the top of the mountain and destroyed homes. They were in need of a hero to bring them relief and safety. Miobe took on the challenge, thinking he had nothing to lose and everything to gain. He started up the mountain, and a monster who was as big as a Chinese barge came out of his cave, spewing fire everywhere. Miobe ran down the hill to get away from the flames. When Miobe stopped and looked back up the hill, he saw that the monster was as big as five Chinese barges. Not understanding, Miobe took a deep breath, closed his eyes, and ran to the top of the mountain. When he reached the top, he saw only a tiny creature, the size of a kitten. Miobe picked it up. It spewed a puff of smoke. Cradling the creature, Miobe returned to the village triumphant.

Someone asked the monster its name. The creature responded, "My name is Fear."

~

Optional Stories

"The Emperor's New Clothes" Denmark. Andersen, H. C., Hersholt, J., & Kredel, F. (1949). *The Complete Andersen: All of the 168 Stories by Hans Christian Anderson.* New York: Heritage Press.

"Iron John" (Germany). Grimm, J., & Grimm, W. (1987). *The Complete Fairy Tales of the Brothers Grimm* (J. Zipes,Trans.). New York: Bantam.

"Rough Face Girl" (Algonquin Indian). Martin, R. (1992). *Rough-Face Girl, The.* G.P. Putnam's Sons.

"Three Scholars and a Lion" (India). Meade, E. H. (2001). *The Moon in the Well: Wisdom Tales to Transform Your Life, Family, and Community.* Chicago, IL: Open Court.

"Truth, Falsehood, Wind, and Fire" (Ethiopia). Bennett, W. J. (1996). *The Book of Virtues: A Treasury of Great Moral Stories.* New York: Simon & Schuster.

Note: An online search will often lead to a printed text of the above stories.

 **NOTES**

∼ NOTES ∼

THE SIXTH STEP

*Were entirely ready to have God remove
all these defects of character*

SOMETIMES IT'S REALLY DIFFICULT TO LOOK AT OURSELVES and realize that, yes, sometimes we were wrong and someone else was right. Sometimes the very same behavior that served us in the past became the very thing that put us in a position to be hurt, embarrassed, scrutinized, criticized, reprimanded or even arrested. So we consider, is it really important to be right? Or is it more important to own our part in creating the problem?

THE MAN WHO WENT LOOKING FOR LUCK
A Greek folktale

There was once a young man who had a chip on his shoulder, a huge chip on his shoulder made of resentments, missed opportunities, and second-place finishes. Everywhere he looked, people were succeeding. They had everything that he wanted and thought he deserved. Jealous of those who seemed to have it all, he decided it must because he had had a run of bad luck. There was only one solution. He needed to have a chat with God and find out where his luck was.

He woke up one day, grabbed his backpack, and headed to the mountaintop, for that is where one goes to find God. He went up that mountain without any thought to the empty soda cans and candy wrappers he was throwing into the forest. He was oblivious to the flowers that died beneath his boots. He was so oblivious to his surroundings that he tripped over a wolf lying prostrate in the path. The wolf appeared to be dying.

"Wolf! Whattsa matter you?"

"I haven't eaten in days, and I'm dying! Can't you see that?"

The wolf moaned in pain.

The young man found that pathetic. "Sucks to be you."

"Man, help me."

"Nah. I'm on my way to see God. Need to have a chat with The Man and find out where my luck is. But I will ask Him where your next meal is coming from. See ya!" And off he went.

The young man continued up the mountain, thinking only of how he was going to give God a piece of his mind. It just wasn't fair to be deprived of the good things in life. He was rehearsing his speech to God, and not paying attention to where he was going. He tripped over the roots of a very large tree that was leaning precariously to the west. The tree was creaking out loud.

"Tree! Whattsa matter you?"

"I can't seem to stand straight and tall. I'm afraid I'll fall over and crush the house where the farmer and his family live. They could be killed! Could you take an axe to my trunk and chop me down so I don't hurt them?"

"Nah. I'm going to have a chat with God. Sorry. I gotta give God a piece of my mind, gotta find out where my luck is. But what I will do is find out why you can't stand up straight. See ya!" And off he went.

The young man continued his trek up the mountain and stopped when he heard someone sobbing uncontrollably. It was a young woman, crying her eyes out.

"Lady, whattsa matter you?"

"My fiancé was killed in the war. Life just isn't worth living anymore. I'll never love anyone again!" There was silence for a few moments. "Will you sit with me for a while?"

"Nah. I'm on my way to see God. Tell him what I think of the way He's running things, and find out where my luck is. But what I will do is find out if you will find love again. See ya!" And off he went.

Finally, the young man got to the mountaintop. "God! Where are you? Where's my luck? Everybody else seems to have good luck and good fortune, too. Where's mine?"

And God answered. "My son, luck is all around you. All you have to do is keep your eyes open, and you will find your luck. If you do that, you will get everything you want and everything you deserve. Now, about your friends ..." God gave the man messages for the wolf, the tree, and the young woman. The young man, charged with enthusiasm, went barreling down the mountain. He stopped at the tree where the young woman was still sitting, weeping quietly.

"Lady, Lady! I talked to God. He says you will love again. As a matter of fact, God said the next man to cross your path will be the love of your life! How's that for good news!"

"It's wonderful news!" She sidled closer to him and looked into his eyes. She tucked her hand around his arm. "Would you like to come into the house for some lunch? Please?"

"Oh no. I've got to find my luck. God says it's all around me, and I have to keep my eyes open. See ya!" And off he went. He was running down the mountain so fast, he tripped over the very same roots that had tripped him up before. The young man fell flat on his face. The oak tree was still leaning to the west and creaking.

"Tree, you've got to do something about those roots! As a matter of fact, God says those roots are your whole trouble. Well, not exactly the roots, but what's in the roots. God said there's a pot of leprechaun gold that got buried in your roots, and now it's causing you to lean to the West. All you need is someone to dig it up for you, and you'll right yourself in no time."

"Wow. Y'know, there's a shovel just inside the barn. If you dig up the gold, you can have it. Really. I have no use for gold. Just go get the shovel. I'd be mighty grateful."

"Nah. I got to find my luck. God said it's all around me, and I just have to keep my eyes open to find it. See ya!" And off he went, leaping over fallen trees and boulders, but falling over the wolf.

"Wolf, I saw God. And God told me that I would get everything I deserved. All I have to do is keep my eyes open, and I'll find my luck. By the way, God said that you should eat the next fool to cross your path."

And the wolf did.

~

Discussion of "The Man Who Went Looking for Luck"
As It Relates to the Sixth Step

This is a cautionary tale about being ignorant of one's own character. This young man is comparing his insides to someone else's outsides, simply because he isn't ready to look at himself. He

∼ NOTES ∼

THE SEVENTH STEP

Humbly Asked Him to remove our shortcomings.

ARE YOU IMPATIENT? Would you like to be more patient? Be careful what you wish for! If we pray for patience, we will be given ample opportunity to practice having patience! Are you unduly suspicious and judgmental of others? Would you like to be more tolerant and forgiving? Careful! Praying for tolerance of others may put scary or obnoxious human beings in your path so you may practice tolerance and forgiveness. But after a bit of practice being patient and tolerant, our shortcomings are transformed into assets once we ask for Divine help and get out of our own way.

HIDDEN AND DUDDEN AND DONALD O'NEARY
An Irish Folktale

Donald O'Neary and his mama lived on a little bitty strip of land and had one cow.

Donald fancied himself a farmer, but Donald was dumb. He was so dumb he couldn't master his letters or colors or numbers. He tried, but could only ever count to six. His mama did teach him to say his prayers every night. They would get down on their knees, clasp their hands to their chests and pray, "Oh, please, dear God. Send my poor wee Donald a thought!" Nothing ever happened, but it didn't matter. Each night, Donald and his mama would ask.

One day, as all mamas do, Donald's mama died. The people of the town helped him make the arrangements to bury his mama. After the funeral, Donald sat alone in his house. He remembered what his mama had taught him. He got down on his knees, clasped his hands to his chest, and prayed out loud, "Oh, please dear God, send me a thought!" But nothing happened.

Each day, Donald would get up and tend his cow, Daisy. He would sit on the porch and watch the grass grow. There was a lot of grass to watch, for on each side of Donald's land was a farm; a huge farm. The farm to the east was owned by Hudden, and the one to the west belonged to Dudden. They wanted to combine their land into one huge farm that could hold four hundred head of cattle. However, Donald's land ran right in between the two farms. Hudden and Dudden had been scheming to get Donald's land for years, but had never figured out how to do it.

Killing Donald's cow would solve the problem. Surely Donald would sell his land to them once he had no cow! The two conspirators crept over the fence and killed Daisy. When Donald saw his beloved Daisy lying dead, he dropped to his knees, clasped his hands to his chest and prayed out loud, "Oh, please dear God, send me a thought!" And God did.

Donald skinned his beloved cow, but had no idea what to do with the carcass. He left it for the birds, and scraped the hide until it was clean and soft. He laid the hide in the yard so it could tan in the sun. When it was a fine piece of leather, Donald took all the coins out of his penny jar, and put them in the hide. After Donald tied the ends of the hide, he put a tiny slit in the leather, put the bag over his shoulder and went into town.

His first stop was the pub. Donald hadn't had a decent meal since mama died. Donald ordered the most expensive dinner they had, which got the owner's attention. "How do you plan to pay for your supper?"

"I've got a magic hide that gives me all the money I want." Donald shook the hide over the table, and a penny fell out. Another shake, another penny. A series of rapid shakes brought a stream of pennies onto the table. The pub owner's eyes grew wide.

"How much for that magic hide?"

"It's not for sale."

"Now, Donald, every man has his price. How much?"

Donald didn't bat an eye. "Its weight in gold." The pub's owner brought out scales and some gold. The hide was weighed, and Donald went home with a large chunk of change.

Donald sat down on his front porch, and proceeded to count out his money. It was a challenge, because Donald could only count to six. But Donald made piles of six gold coins, and then counted the piles up to six. Each group of six piles became a big pile. And he counted the big piles up to six. And so on. Donald was having a wonderful time! Hudden and Dudden took notice.

"Where did you get all that money?"

"Don't you know that cow's hides are fetching their weight in gold?"

No further encouragement was needed. Hudden and Dudden went into their pastures, slaughtered all their cattle, left the carcasses for the birds. They tanned the cow's hides until they were soft leather. They loaded the hides into a wagon and went into town, intending to make a fortune. The pub's owner saw them coming, and assuming they were partners with Donald O'Neary, called them "swindlers and charlatans." Then the owner assaulted them, and demanded a refund. There was such a commotion that the constable ran Hudden and Dudden out of town. They were furious, and vowed to get even with Donald O'Neary.

That night, Hudden and Dudden sewed several of the hides together. They snuck into Donald's house and, with a large club, knocked Donald unconscious. They put Donald into the leather sheet, tied it up, and put a stout pole through it. Hudden put one end of the pole on his shoulder, Dudden took the other. Together, they made their way towards the river. They were going to get rid of that Donald O'Neary once and for all.

When the sun came up, Hudden and Dudden were mighty hungry. Stopping for breakfast seemed like a good idea, as it was still several miles to the river. Donald, still unconscious from the blow to the head, was left in the leather sack outside the pub. While Hudden and Dudden were stuffing their faces and wetting their whistles, Donald woke up in a panic. There was a large goose egg on the back of his head. Donald remembered what his mama taught him to do. He scooted around in that leather bag until he was on his knees. He clasped his hands to his chest, and he prayed, "Oh please, dear God, send me a thought!" And He did. Donald began to shout.

"I'll not marry her. No, no, no. Not for all the money in the world. Not for half the kingdom! I'll not marry her, I tell you. I'll not do it!" A young farmer who was headed to market with four hundred head of cattle stopped in his tracks. He approached the leather sack.

"You'll not marry who, might I ask?"

"Why, the princess! I wouldn't marry her if my life depended on it. Not for all the money in the world. Not for half the kingdom."

"Well, I'd marry her." The young farmer peered inside the leather sack. "You would?"

"For all that money? And half the kingdom? Sure I would! Could I trade places with you?" "What's in it for me?"

"I've got four hundred head of cattle that I was going to sell at the market today. I'm not going to need them or the money from that sale. You're more than welcome to them."

Donald thought that was a good trade. After they traded places, Donald walked to the front of the herd of cows and led them home. When he opened the gate into his tiny strip of land, the force of the cows trying to fit into the space burst the fences to Hudden's farm and Dudden's farm. Suddenly, there was one huge farm with four hundred head of cattle grazing contentedly in front of Donald's house. Donald had great fun trying to count them all. It took a while, since he could only count to six.

Meanwhile, Hudden and Dudden came out of the pub two sheets to the wind. They stumbled over to the leather bag with the farmer inside, and hoisted it up. When they got to river's edge, they flung that leather bag into the water and watched it sink. That was the end of Donald O'Neary. Or so they thought.

It was just about sunset when Hudden and Dudden were walking up the lane to their farms. A shadowy figure was lurking on Donald's porch. Donald's ghost seeking revenge? Slowly they crept to Donald's porch. That was no ghost! It was Donald himself! They lunged at Donald, but Donald put up his hands and just grinned.

"Hmmmm … fraud … and kidnapping … and murder. What would the Constable say?" Hudden and Dudden cowered. "I've a mind to call the Constable. But if you promise to be good to me, I'll let you work on my farm." Hudden and Dudden had no choice but to accept. That night, Donald gave thanks for the inspired thoughts that brought him four hundred cows and two seasoned cowboys named Hudden and Dudden.

$$\sim$$

Discussion of "Hudden and Dudden and Donald O'Neary" As It Relates to the Seventh Step

Donald O'Neary knows that he is dumb. He's had lots of evidence to support that belief.

And while "dumb" isn't a character defect so much as an accident of birth, being dumb does hamper his ability to function in the world. Donald's mama gave him "Good Orderly Direction," so that when Donald faced a dilemma, he had no qualms about asking for Divine help. Donald asked for divine help on a regular basis, with no expectation of the outcome.

Donald's story is a beautiful example of "God may or may not answer when you want Him to, but he always answers on time." For years, Donald and his mama asked that Donald be given a thought. And for years, all they did was ask. When push came to shove, Donald was given an intuitive thought that guided his actions. Donald took what was given and put one foot in front of the other to make progress through his dilemmas. Donald's blind faith that he would get the answers he needed held him in good stead. By story's end, Donald had a life beyond his wildest dreams.

Donald's story bears witness to the fact that the Twelve Step Design does not provide instant results and that it is progress, not perfection that we seek. Whether Donald's actions were that of an honorable man is a question for discussion and debate.

~

Exploring Personal Shortcomings and Personal Responsibility

1.   Donald's actions are based on a need to survive hardship. Does that hardship give him permission to do whatever he needs to do to survive?

2.   What motivated Donald to share the secret of his sudden wealth with Hudden and Dudden? Did Donald purposely set them up for failure?

3.   Discuss what it means to have "blind faith." Does that level of faith take away the need for taking any action to improve our circumstances? Does having faith excuse us from taking personal responsibility for our actions?

4.   Are Donald's actions those of an honorable man? Is he getting rich due to a con game and blackmail? Is that acceptable behavior?

5.   How does the death of Donald's mother force him to grow? Would she be proud of him?

6. Donald certainly experiences humiliation in the beginning of this story. What does it mean to be humiliated? What does it mean to be humble? Does Donald ever become humble?

7. How many examples of people who wanted something for nothing do we find in the story? How destructive can greed be when it becomes one's motivation? Do you see examples of greed motivating destructive actions in your world?

~

For the Storyteller

My adaptation of this story is based on two variants of the tale. I first found it in *Irish Folk Tales*, edited by Henry Glassie. There are detailed notes about the origins of this story in that publication. I also used Jeremiah Curtain's variant found in *Myths and Folklore of Ireland*, first published in 1890. An earlier version is known as "The Ploughman's Tale" may be found in Geoffery Chaucer's *Canterbury Tales*. It is AT Tale type 1535 with versions found in Italy, Germany, and Denmark.

~

Synopsis of the story

Donald O'Neary lived with his mother on a small plot of land that could only support one cow. Donald had never been very smart, and his mother wanted him to be smart and successful. She knew it would take Divine intervention to help her son, so she prayed, and taught him to pray, for help. Their neighbor, Hudden and Dudden, wanted that piece of land so that they could combine resources and become very rich. After Donald's mother died, the neighbors killed Donald's cow, thinking Donald would sell his land or abandon it. Donald did neither. He prayed for help and got an idea that would let him appear rich and successful. When his cow was killed, he used the hide to create the illusion of magically produced wealth. Hudden and Dudden's greed led them to try and duplicate Donald's success. However, they did not experience the same success, so they wanted revenge. In the dead of night, they knocked Donald out and tied him up so they could drown him in the river.

Getting Donald to the river required a long hike. Both Hudden and Dudden required food and drink before they could complete the task. While they stopped for food and drink, Donald prayed for guidance and escaped death by conning a young farmer into trading places with him in exchange for four hundred head of cattle. Hudden and Dudden resumed their trek, assuming that the body they carried was Donald's. Having no clue it wasn't Donald whom they threw into the river, the two men returned to their farms expecting to merge their two farms into one.

Awaiting their return was Donald, having laid claim to both of their farms. Before the men could retaliate, Donald threatened to turn Hudden and Dudden in to the authorities for kidnapping and murder. To avoid prosecution and incarceration, Hudden and Dudden ended up working for Donald.

〜

Optional Stories

"The Perfect Wife" (Traditional Nasrudin Tale). Kornfield, Jack, and Christina Feldman, eds. *Soul Food: Stories to Nourish the Spirit and the heart*. San Francisco: HarperSanFrancisco, 1996.

"The Silent Couple" (Ireland). Glassie, H. (Ed.). (1985). *Irish Folk Tales*. NY: Pantheon Books.

"The Envious Neighbor" (Japan). Lang, A. (1966). *Violet Fairy Book*. NY: Dover Publications.

"The Twelve Months" (Germany). Grimm, J., & Grimm, W. (1987). *The Complete Fairy Tales of the Brothers Grimm* (J. Zipes, Trans.). New York: Bantam.

"Coyote and Wasichu" (Native American). E., & Ortiz, A. (1984). *American Indian Myths and Legends*. New York: Pantheon Books.

"Coyote, Iktome, and the Rock" (Native American). E., & Ortiz, A. (1984). *American Indian Myths and Legends*. New York: Pantheon Books.

"The Heifer Hide" (Southern Appalachian). Chase, Richard, and Berkeley Williams. *The Jack Tales*. New York: Houghton Mifflin Company, 2003.

Note: An online search will often lead to a printed text of the above stories.

∽ NOTES ∽

∼ NOTES ∼

THE EIGHTH AND NINTH STEPS

Step Eight: Made a list of all persons we had harmed and were willing to make amends to them all.

Step Nine: Made direct amends wherever possible, except when to do so would injure them or others.

STEPS EIGHT AND NINE SUGGEST THAT WE CLEAN UP the damage from our active addictions and remove the regret, remorse, shame, and guilt that have fueled the addiction. Sometimes it's hard to know who has been hurt. Sometimes it's even harder to take responsibility for having caused the damage. Sometimes it's just too big a mountain to climb. Rest assured, there is no deadline for the completion of these steps. Being aware of the harm caused, and the willingness to correct it, will open the door of opportunity.

LIKE MEAT LOVES SALT
A Folktale from India

The king was in his wine cellar after the birth of his youngest. He had just left the Queen's chambers after holding his newest child, a daughter. She was perfect in every way. Tiny, pink, ten fingers, ten toes, curly red hair atop a perfectly formed head. Just moments before, she was marveling at the babe's beauty when the midwife screamed. The Queen was dead. An animal-like scream came from the King's gullet, and he fled the Queen's chambers. He sought refuge in the wine cellar. How was he to be both mother and father to three small girls? How would the affairs of the castle be tended without his wife's firm but gentle hand? To whom could he trust his children while he attended affairs of state? Tonight, he sought solace in his wine cellar, not knowing if he was mourning his Queen or celebrating his precious third daughter.

He was, by all accounts, a good king. He always put the needs of his subject high above his own, and made many personal sacrifices for the good of his kingdom. When his borders were threatened, he led his own troops into battle, and fought beside the best and the worst of his knights. He had been known for his celebrations of victories, holy days, and harvest moons, when the food was plentiful, and the wine flowed freely. If one of his subjects was in need of his wisdom or his justice, he would stop whatever he was doing and attend to that issue. His justice was swift, and based on a code of absolutes that left no room for debate or doubt. But the cost of such justice on the King's soul was high, and often the King took refuge in the wine cellars of the castle after such a trial.

The King left the raising of his children to the queen's ladies, expecting his three daughters would be raised to understand the demands of his office. He assumed they would teach the princesses wifely and queenly duties and demeanors. Without his beloved, the King threw himself into the duties of his office, attending his daughters as if his wife had lived. Then, he would only be expected to make his appearance in the nursery to tell a story, or at the very least, kiss his children good-night. He marveled at their innocence and told himself that he was a good father.

But when the King's calendar was cleared for his daughters, he lavished the great resources of his treasury on them to make up for his absence. He asked nothing more than their undying devotion and loyalty to him and to him alone. Each gift, each gesture, each token was an attempt to soothe his guilty conscience. The older girls understood this and their father's need to be adored, especially when he emerged from the wine cellar.

The older sisters planned and plotted their way into their father's heart. They asked for gifts costly and rare which they accepted with hollow words of love and obedience. He believed they loved him truly and without reservation, and so, he continued to bestow gifts upon them believing the gifts were enough. The older girls quickly learned how to get the very best of everything from their father.

The youngest girl didn't understand how her sisters could be so heartless. She really did love he father without reservation, and didn't really care for the baubles he bestowed upon her. She knew that how she received them was of utmost importance to His Majesty. There were rages of temper when he thought she wasn't pleased. It was as though the size of his gifts were to fill the size of the hole in her father's heart, not hers. The princess simply wanted her father's time and attention. But she participated in the empty ritual, hoping for more.

The King's duties defined him, and there was no time to find, much less court, a queen who might bear him a son. As the years passed, it became clearer and clearer that the King needed to choose one of the three princesses as his heir. As he loved them all as much as he was capable, he was loath to decide which daughter would be so favored as to become the Queen. Understanding that the fate of his old age would be left to the daughter who would become the Queen, he posed this question to each of the children.

"How much do you love me?"

"I love you beyond what can be valued as rich or rare," spoke the eldest daughter.

The King was pleased, knowing that both his kingdom and his old age would be in good hands. He only had to look at his middle child who volunteered, "I love you no less than life itself."

Smiling, the King understood that his second daughter would protect him as she would protect the kingdom when he was no longer capable. Facing a most difficult choice, the King turned to his youngest.

"I love you as meat loves salt."

The King's face grew red. "SALT??? Common table salt? Salt shows only the sensibility of a peasant, not the sensibility of a king! You don't love me at all! Get out! Go as far as your feet will carry you and never return to the palace!"

The youngest princess fled to her chambers and cried as she felt her heart break. But to ignore a royal command would be certain death, so she dressed in the clothes of one of the kitchen maids, made a bundle of her jewels, and left the place where she had been born to face an uncertain future in a world she didn't know. Her father fled to the wine cellar, and drank as he felt his heart break. He had just made his youngest child an orphan. He drank until he slept.

The princess walked until she became tired. She saw an inn and hoped to stay there, but when she looked about, she saw rowdy men and the equally rowdy women who served them. She didn't feel safe. Frantically, she looked around the room, hoping to see some goodness in someone's face. She tiptoed about the great hall, and peered into the kitchen. Cook was standing by the hearth, stirring a kettle of soup while the serving girls hollered for this meal and that. Cook casually wiped her brow, and served up the soup with a smile. The princess walked into the kitchen and offered to help cook in exchange for a night's lodging.

Cook just nodded. The princess stood beside the cook and simply took over the tending of the soup. Not a word was spoken, but the princess knew that she was safe in Cook's domain.

At the palace, a lesson in matters of state began in earnest. But if the King tried to explain some matter of diplomacy, his elder daughters grew impatient or bored. Understanding the workings of the kingdom's economy was essential to the well-being and security of the land, so including his daughters in those decisions would give them some background in finance.

They needed to be able to make sound decisions. But the older princesses were only interested in the household expenses, lacking the vision to appreciate the complexity of governing a nation. The King had become acutely aware of how much his youngest child meant to him.

Teaching her to follow in his footsteps would have been a far different experience than educating her siblings. The baby of the family loved learning for its own sake, and took delight in mastering a complex equation or theory. His Royal Highness missed her gentle, undemanding ways, especially in light of the royal wedding and the coronation of her sister that was to follow. His eldest's demands taxed the King's patience and his treasury, and the King began to think he had acted far too harshly when he banished his youngest. But what was done was done. The King had little choice but to take refuge in the wine cellar and accept the consequences of those actions that sent his baby girl into the kingdom as an orphan.

Meanwhile, the princess had become a great help to Cook, never complaining and always asking to do more. Cook taught the young lass to create delicate soups and stews. The princess learned to make breads, cookies, and pastries worthy of the King's table. The inn's reputation for fine food quickly spread throughout the kingdom, so when the King's eldest daughter and heir to the throne were to be married, the Cook and her young assistant were asked to prepare the wedding feast.

The princess was thrilled. At least she would be able to participate in her sister's wedding! She would see her family and witness the great event from afar, even though she could not be a member of the wedding party and sit at the Royal table. She collaborated with Cook on the menu, skillfully suggesting all of the King's favorite dishes for the royal feast. The two women worked tirelessly around the clock, making sure that each and every morsel was perfect. The princess was responsible for making the King's favorite dish, and she made it without salt.

At last, the day of the Royal Wedding arrived. In spite of his misgivings, the King beamed as he walked his eldest daughter down the aisle. She was married with great ceremony in a most lavish and public setting. Everything seemed to be perfect. Once all the guests were seated in the castle's great hall, the King led his eldest, now the Queen, and her Consort, to the head table, playing the gracious host, the proud father, and the benevolent monarch all at once. The meal was served. One course after another was served. Each was met with great anticipation ... and then words of high praise for the cook who had created it. At last, the King's favorite meat dish was served. The King lifted his fork high with relish, mouth watering at the thought, and then...his face turned red with rage as he spat the food across the table. "This is without taste! It has been ruined! Stop the platters from being passed! Summon that cook!!! The princess, still in her cook's apron, entered the great hall and approached the King. "You have ruined my favorite meat. By doing so, you have ruined the wedding feast!!!"

The princess bowed deeply to her father. "Have mercy, your majesty, and please forgive me. I once heard from the King's own mouth that, 'Salt shows only the sensibility of a peasant, not the sensibility of a King!' How could I have dared to mix salt with your meat?"

The silence in the room was deafening. All eyes were on the King, his face flushed with shame. The King recognized the words as his own, and the cook as his own youngest child.

Everyone held his breath as the King rose and went to face the cook. As he got closer to her, his eyes filled with tears. He lifted her to her feet. His voice broke as he uttered these words. "It is, indeed, the salt that brings out the best in the meat. And it is you, my child, who brings out the best in me. Please forgive me and come home."

There was an audible gasp from the crowd. The youngest princess had been presumed dead by the citizens of that kingdom. And yet, here she was, having prepared and served the marriage feast to the family who had banished her. Slowly, the princess raised her face to meet her father's gaze. They stood, toe to toe, eye to eye. She looked deep into his eyes, searching for some acknowledgment of her suffering that had been caused by her father's command.

Tears filled with remorse streaked the King's face as he opened his arms, entreating his youngest to come back into the fold. When she stepped into his embrace, both father and daughter wept. The crowd came to its feet and cheered, giving voice to their relief.

Then the King escorted his youngest daughter to the Royal Table, seated her at his side, and made a toast in her honor. With a wave of the royal scepter, the celebration resumed with even greater joy.

～

Discussion of "Like Meat Loves Salt"
As It Relates to the Eighth and Ninth Steps

Denial is the best friend of the alcoholic/addict. One of the most common excuses about one's active drinking and drugging is, "I'm only hurting myself." There are other myths as well. "I go to work every day … My family has everything they need … I give them everything they want." There is another myth that the absence of the alcoholic/addict is preferable, given the havoc the addicted person has brought into the home. Sadly, the alcoholic/addict truly believes such myths until they begin the process of recovery.

Such is the case with the King. He sees himself as the victim in this family, having been cruelly abandoned by his spouse. He cannot stand his own pain, much less his daughters', so he numbs his heart with alcohol. The King can convince himself that his offspring are fine because they have everything they need in the way of food, clothing, and shelter. Sadly, he doesn't understand that his girls need him, and yes, he has hurt them deeply.

What his daughters know is that they are not worthy of their father's time and attention. His majesty is blissfully unaware of the harm he has done his youngest child until he is publicly humiliated at the wedding feast. His youngest child parrots the King's own words and forces him to see how much harm he has done. The apology that he delivers publicly, while important, isn't enough.

Making direct amends means righting the wrong, and healing the harm done. Making amends is often a process, especially in families. It is often a difficult process, and may require professional help. But healing is possible if the recovering person, as well as the family, is willing to walk through the discomfort of taking responsibility for the past. Beyond that lies forgiveness, and learning how to live in harmony, peace, and love.

~

Exploring of the Role of Forgiveness in Relationships

1.   Sketch or draw the part of the story that speaks to you. Share how you connected to the story at that point.

2.   Have a discussion defining the differences between needs and wants. Which needs were fulfilled in the royal family? Which were not? How does one get their needs does met in recovery and in adulthood when they were not met in childhood?

3.   There is a tendency to assume that because a family has sufficient financial resources that the family is healthy and happy. There is also a belief that if one looks good and presents well, that person is healthy, happy, and fully functional.

Using the royal family of the story, dismantle those assumptions. Without using names, compare this family to other families you know?

4.   Using the dynamic of the alcoholic family, identify which role each member of the royal family assumes. (Woititz, J. G. (1983). *Adult Children of Alcoholics*. Pompano Beach, Fla.: Health Communications.) With which character do you relate most closely?

5.   Many people in recovery need to "find their voice" and assert themselves for the first time. With whom do you need to share your hurt? Is there someone that you have hurt who is deserving of amends or a second chance?

6.   Second chances are a theme throughout the recovery community. Who deserves a second chance? Is there any reason why a second chance would be inappropriate or foolhardy?

～

For the Storyteller

This is the story on which William Shakespeare's *The Tragedy of King Lear* is based. A little research yields versions of this story in France, Germany, Austria, and Italy. There are also versions found in India and Pakistan. My adaptation is based on "The Most Indispensable Thing" translated from the German folktale by D.L. Ashilman, and "The Necessity of Salt" also translated by D.L. Ashilman from the Austrian. It is AT Tale type 923.

~

Synopsis

The Queen dies in childbirth after delivering her third daughter. The King is distraught, and seeks relief from his grief by drinking. He fails to make the necessary changes to become a single parent, assuming that the Queen's ladies will do the necessary child rearing. The King is absent from his daughter's lives. While he feels quite guilty about not being a good father, he does little to correct the situation other than giving the girls whatever material thing they want.

To mask his feeling of inadequacy, he drinks a great deal. Suddenly, the King finds himself old and needing an heir. As he never remarried to sire a son, he must choose one of his daughters to be the heir to the kingdom. He asks, "How much do you love me?" thinking the best answer deserves the crown. The elder daughters both give lofty responses about their love. The youngest says, "I love you as meat loves salt," and is immediately banished.

She makes her way out of the castle and into the world, seeking sanctuary with the cook of the local inn.

While under the cook's protection, the princess becomes a culinary marvel. As a result of the princess' talents, the inn becomes quite prosperous and well known. The King calls upon the cook and her assistant to prepare the wedding feast for his eldest daughter who will become the Queen. The princess, in her new role as a chef, prepares His Majesty's favorite meat without salt. At the feast, the King is incensed that the meat is prepared without salt—or taste. He calls for the young chef to admonish and humiliate her in public. When she hears his displeasure, she gives him his own words, that "salt shows the sensibility of a peasant, not a king." The King realizes who stands in front of him, and how his words have created pain and unnecessary suffering. He welcomes his daughter back into the Royal Family, and the celebration resumes with greater joy than before.

∽

Optional Stories

"Clever Manka" (Jewish American). Schram, Peninnah. *Jewish Stories One Generation Tells Another.* Lanham: Rowman & Littlefield Publishers, 2005.

"Goose Girl at the Spring." Collected by the Brothers Grimm, Grimm, Jacob, and Wilhelm Grimm. *The Complete Fairy Tales of the Brothers Grimm.* Trans. Jack Zipes. New York: Bantam, 1987.

"Meat of the Tongue" (Kenya Mi). Friedman, Amy, and Jillian Hulme Gilliland. *The Spectacular Gift and Other Tales from Tell Me a Story.* Kansas City, MO: Andrews and McMeel,

1995.

"Buffalo Woman" (Native American). Goble, Paul. *Buffalo Woman*. NY: Atheneum , 1984.

Note: An online search will often lead to a printed text of the above stories.

∽ NOTES ∽

～ NOTES ～

THE TENTH STEP

*Continued to take personal inventory, and
when we were wrong, promptly admitted it.*

THE TENTH STEP IS THE FIRST of the maintenance steps, encouraging us to make the leap from learning the program to living the program. In that process, we learn compassion, tolerance, and forgiveness as a way of interacting with the world. We learn to walk a mile in the other man's moccasins, and relationships are no longer disposable. Relationships are precious and need care, as Leah demonstrates in this next tale.

LEAH'S LAUNDRY
A Jewish Folktale

Several hundred years ago, washing clothes was an arduous task. It was back-breaking work that took the better part of a day. A woman named Leah had just spent six hours washing clothes. Sweat dripped from her hairline into her eyelashes and continued down her neck. Her back ached, and the skin on her hands was taut and dry. Several clotheslines spanned the courtyard that she shared with her neighbors. Slowly and carefully, Leah hung the wash out to dry on the lines. She was careful not to let the clean clothes touch the ground, lest they become soiled again. Once the laundry had been hung to dry, Leah looked at how clean and bright it was. Satisfied with a job well done, she went into her house to rest.

Ariela, Leah's neighbor, lived just across the shared courtyard. On this particular day, Ariela had gone to the marketplace to hear the news of the day and to purchase honey and spices. She paid for the honey, cardamom, and cumin she needed, and pocketed the change. As she wandered through the market, she enjoyed the sight of exquisite silks, rubies that sparkled in the sun, and the sounds of children playing games in the streets. When the sun shifted to the West, Ariela started to walk back to her village. She put her hand in her pocket expecting to feel the half-shekels that were her change from her purchase. They were gone. Frantically Ariela searched her other pockets, and her bundle of goods looking for her monies. The money was really gone.

Ariela began to mutter to herself, berating herself for her carelessness. She worried about the reaction of her husband once she revealed the loss. She predicted an argument erupting into violent words and perhaps even violent actions. Her children didn't need to witness that again. With each step, she became more and more afraid to cross the threshold of her house. Not wanting to be seen by a soul, she walked with her head down, and made a beeline for her front door. She was smacked in the face with Leah's wet laundry.

"AAUUUGHHH!" Ariela began beating the woolen fabric out of her face. " Not only have I lost my money, but I am also hit in the face with someone's wet wool drawers! AAUUGGH!" Frustrated and angry, Ariela fought with the clothes, stormed into her house, grabbed a pair of scissors, cut the clothesline, and left all that fresh laundry in the dirt of the courtyard. She stomped into her house and slammed the door.

The commotion sent Leah to her window. Leah saw all of her freshly laundered clothes and bedclothes lying in the dust of the courtyard. Six hours of backbreaking work ruined. Leah screamed. "Oh NO!!!!! All that work...for nothing!!! What is the matter with that woman?! What gives her the right...???" Leah had worked herself into a rage. Then Leah got quiet and began muttering under her breath. "We'll see about that. When she hangs her fresh laundry out and finds it in the dirt, she'll see how it feels! Vengeance will be MINE!" As Leah picked up the dirty laundry, the tears began to flow. Soon she was sobbing.

Then, she stopped. Leah took a deep breath. In fact, she took several. In that brief pause, she said to herself, "They tell me that everything happens for a reason. I don't understand why it had to be my clothes that ended up in the dirt. But there they are. Dirty. Not my doing. Not my fault ..." Another voice seemed to say, "Now Leah, go fix that stupid clothesline, wash the dirt off the soiled pieces, and re-hang the laundry." So she did. Some items had to be washed again. Some did not. When everything was again clean and fresh, Leah hung her clothes back up to dry. That evening, when she brought the laundry inside, Leah was amazed to find that she was in a good mood. She was in such a good mood that she forgot to mention the incident to her husband.

Ariela waited for Leah to pound on her door, demanding at the very least, an explanation, or some sort of restitution, or at the very worst, revenge. But Leah didn't come pound on her door. She simply cleaned up the mess that Ariela had made. This baffled Ariela, and made her more and more uncomfortable ... and ashamed. Leah had done nothing to provoke such anger. Ariela's misfortune had nothing to do with Leah's laundry. Guilt and remorse overcame Ariela. Soon, Ariela felt like she was going to jump out of her skin. She had no choice but to walk across the courtyard to Leah's house.

Ariela knocked on the door and waited. When Leah opened the door, there was an awkward silence. The words burst forth out of Ariela's mouth. "Leah, I'm so sorry. I acted like I was crazy. I don't know what possessed me." The two women sat down, and Ariela shared the story of her day, the loss of money, and the frustration that she took out on Leah's laundry.

Leah forgave Ariela. She also let Ariela know that the story of her bad behavior had been kept a secret. Leah hadn't shared it with a soul, not even her husband. It was not, and never would be, fodder for gossip.

Now it was Ariela's turn to be stunned. "Thank you."

Leah smiled. "Having a good neighbor is so much more important than clean laundry."

~

Discussion of "Leah's Laundry"
As It Relates to the Tenth Step

It's really hard to admit when one is wrong, because the admission requires vulnerability. Self-righteous anger is much more fun. There's an adrenalin rush, a sense of invincibility, and a power surge that can lead to rage. Unfortunately, rage does damage, much like the damage done in active addiction. Innocent bystanders get caught in the tirade, drowned by the tsunami of rage, or bludgeoned by misdirected rage. The fallout is often a damaged or destroyed relationship. At that point, a dose of humble pie becomes the recommended diet so that the relationship can survive, and perhaps even thrive. Beautiful things happen when someone is able to say, "I was wrong and I am sorry." Such is the case with Ariela.

This step also states, "… when we were wrong …" implying that sometimes we aren't. At those times, it is important to not take ownership of a problem that was thrust upon us. It is also important to respond rather than to react in kind. Two wrongs don't make a right. They never did. Such is the case with Leah.

Both women have something to teach us about relationships, and about the benefits of acting quickly and responsibly when something has gone awry.

~

Exploring boundaries and personal responsibility

1. Define "reacting" and "responding." How are they different? Make a listing of the pros and cons of each.

2. Displaced anger and fear can be very ugly, indeed. Why is Ariela afraid? Why does she dump her anger onto Leah's clean clothes? What color is fear? What color is anger? Create a visual representation (drawing or collage) of anger, rage, or fear.

3. In many ways, this story is about not taking things personally, even when the events are awful. What happens in Leah's psyche that allows her to simply clean up the mess Ariela made? How was she able to be the bigger person?

4. There are no adverse consequences for Ariela's behavior.

Is Leah supporting Ariela as a friend, or is she enabling Ariela to continue bad behavior when Leah simply cleans up the mess?

5.   The illustration shows Leah bearing witness to Ariela's pain. Why is bearing witness to the pain so important? How does that differ from helping?

⌒

For the Storyteller

I was looking for stories of forgiveness when I stumbled across "The Clothesline." In the original version, the Rabbi explains to the woman whose laundry had been ruined that everything happens for a reason, and therefore, she was being tested. The Rabbi explained that the experience was to teach restraint. While I loved this idea of this story, I found it difficult to embrace the story as written. I felt the other side of the story was missing. My adaptation adds the story of the woman who performs the angry task, as well as giving names to the two women, thus making it more about the relationship between the two women and less about the Rabbinic perspective of being tested. The original story may be found in *Jewish Tales of Holy Women* by Yitzhak Buxbaum. It is AT Tale Type 910, with similarities to AT Tale Tye 930.

⌒

Synopsis

Leah has just hung her laundry out to dry in the community courtyard when a neighbor walks right into it and is outraged by the inconvenience. The neighbor then gets a knife, and cuts the clothesline down and walks away. Leah's clean laundry is now soiled. Rather than perpetuate the anger, Leah simply repairs the clothesline, re-washes her wash, and hangs it up to dry. Leah's grace shames the neighbor into asking forgiveness. During that conversation, Leah learns the truth about her neighbor's household and the violence within. Leah sees the big picture, and assures her neighbor that her friendship is more important than the laundry.

~

Optional Stories

"The Man who was to Keep the House" (Norway). Dasent, George Webbe. *Popular Tales from Norse Mythology.* Mineola: Dover Publications, 2001.

"The Stubborn Husband & the Stubborn Wife" (Persia). Chinen, Allan B. *Once Upon a Midlife: Classic Stories and Mythic Tales to Illuminate the Middle Years.* Bloomington, IN: Xlibris, 2003.

"Jack the Cunning Thief" (Ireland). Jacobs, Joseph. *Celtic Fairy Tales*, selected and edited by Joseph Jacobs. London: D. Nutt, 1892.

"Rough Faced Girl" (Native American). Martin, Rafe. *Rough-Face Girl, The.* New York: G.P. Putnam's Sons, 1992.

"Just Enough" (Jewish). Pearmain, Elisa Davy. *Doorways to the Soul: 52 Wisdom Tales from Around the World.* Cleveland, OH: Pilgrim Press, 1998.

"The Wolves Within" (Cherokee). http://unbelievableyou.com /a-native-american-cherokee-story-two-wolves/

Note: An online search will often lead to a printed text of the above stories.

∼ NOTES ∼

THE ELEVENTH STEP

Sought though prayer and meditation to improve our conscious contact with God as we understood Him, praying only for the will for us and the power to carry that out.

IT HAS OFTEN BEEN SAID THAT PRAYING is talking to God, and meditation is listening. If those are the only guidelines that have been given, the practice seems daunting, elusive, or entirely too "New Age" to even be considered. The only requirement, as far as I know, is that you stop and be entirely still for a moment, or two, or more. Taking a "time out" from our digitized, homogenized, frenetic pace that has become life as we know it seems a sacrilege.

Paradoxically, that "time out" to connect with our deepest and most innermost selves, and with our concept of the divine, allows us to be centered, grounded, grateful, and at peace.

FRUITS DE MER
A Story to Illustrate Step Eleven
By Beth Ohlsson

Have you ever held a sand dollar in your hand? I collected them as a kid, but I haven't seen one on the beach in decades. I have such lovely memories of collecting them. We would walk on the beach during our annual trek to the ocean, collecting special things to take home and treasure. A sand dollar was rare, but there were lots of jack knife clams, moon shells, angel wings, tetra shells, jingle shells, cockle shells and whelk shells. Some people think whelk shells are called conch shells. They're two different species and look nothing alike, but it didn't matter what they were called. We would collect the shells and run up the beach singing, "Fruits de Mer! Fruits de Mer!" Fruits of the Sea. A gift, a treasure from the ocean to take home and cherish. I had a huge collection of "Fruits de Mer." I displayed it proudly in my bedroom.

One summer, there was a tropical storm that had passed through while we were at the beach. The waves were huge, at least fifteen feet high. The ocean floor had been churned up to such an extent that the "Fruits de Mer" were visible in the wave as they rose high above our heads. We could just run in and snatch up huge whelk shells; just reach up and grab them and call them our own. We would run back to the blanket yelling, "Fruits de Mer! Fruits de Mer!" at the top of our lungs. There must have been a pile of fifty large whelk shells by day's end.

My family went to the beach every single year. Every year, we would scour the beach for the "Fruits de Mer" that had been left just for us. Every year, the choices became fewer and less perfect. But it didn't matter. We loved the sun, the sand, and the surf. We loved the family feasts, and the ban on electronics, and the penny-ante card games played late into the evening. My own sons grew into that annual ritual. From the time they could walk, they would comb the beach shouting "fruits de mer" and claim the treasures that had been left for them. There were few treasures by this time, and what was there was punctuated with discarded plastic bags, soda cans, plastic bottles, cigarette butts, and the occasional condom. But it didn't matter. We still had the sun, the sand and the surf, and all those family rituals.

My mother, who couldn't swim, loved the beach as much as the rest of us. As she aged, the success of the vacation was measured by the number of times we were able to get her down to the water to get her feet wet.

Once the family cottage was gone, those vacations stopped.

Several years later, we planned a family trip to the beach in October. We would once again participate in those precious family rituals. My mother died in September. Despite the sadness, and the fact that our family numbered one less, we decided to go. We had to decide who we were as a family without the matriarch who was the glue that held us together. We did what we knew to do. As the surf crashed onto the shore like it always had, we walked along the beach like we always had. We talked about life without Mom. My heart felt like it was going to burst through my chest. I looked down. Through my tears, I saw a baby whelk shell. Two inches long. Perfect in every way. I picked it up.

"Look! It's a baby! Fruits de Mer! It's going to be okay." I took the whelk shell home.

A month or so later, I found myself at the beach again. This time, I was with a girlfriend. We were walking and talking on the beach. I was sharing about the family reunion at the beach. The tears began to flow unbidden. I looked down and saw a baby starfish. Two inches from point to point. I picked it up.

"Look! It's a baby! Fruits de Mer! It's going to be okay!" I took the starfish home.

Several months later, I was at the beach once more. I was at a conference. Friday night there was a workshop on grief. I said to myself, "Self, you should go. I'm sure you have some unresolved issues surrounding your mother's death. You should go. It will be good for you. Like spinach."

So I went.

There was a speaker who shared that when his father's cancer treatment failed, they had eight days before he passed. The family came from all over the state. Family was getting together, going through scrapbooks, telling stories and family jokes, holding hands. They laughed, they cried, they made their peace and said goodbye. I got angry ... really angry. My mother dropped dead. I didn't get to say goodbye.

The second person who talked said that his mother had decided to refuse all cancer treatment because she wanted to enjoy the time she had left. It turned out she had about eight months. People came from all over the country. Family got together, going through scrapbooks, telling stories and family jokes, holding hands. They laughed, they cried, they made their peace and said goodbye. My blood began to boil. Rage came to the surface. I wanted to scream, "It's not fair! My mommy dropped dead. I didn't get to say goodbye. I don't want to hear it!!!"

I didn't scream. I left.

After all, I was at the beach. I did what I knew to do. I went down to the sand and walked along the surf.

I was walking along the beach. Then I was walking and talking ... to God. Then I was walking and talking and crying to God. Then I was walking and talking and crying and yelling at God that it wasn't fair! I didn't get to say goodbye! Convulsive sobs escaped. I looked down and through my tears I saw a baby sand dollar. I picked it up. I hadn't held a sand dollar in my hand since I was ten. It was the size of a quarter, perfect in every way. I took a few steps and looked down, and there was another sand dollar, about the same size. And then another, and another and another. I was holding five baby sand dollars in my hand; one for each member of my first family. As I stood marveling at these five baby sand dollars in the palm of my hand, a voice said to me very loudly, and very clearly, "If the sea can heal, then so can you."

"Fruits de Mer!"

~

Discussion of "Fruits de Mer" As It Pertains to the Eleventh Step

A relationship with God is a personal and private thing, difficult to put into words, and is the stated purpose of the basic text of Alcoholics Anonymous. I am often guarded when sharing my spiritual experiences for fear of being misunderstood or unfairly diagnosed as having auditory hallucinations. I felt it was appropriate and necessary to share a personal story to illustrate this step, even though it shifts the writing to a different voice. "Fruits de Mer" evolved after my mother died suddenly. At that point, I certainly found myself in a strained relationship with reality. It had simply never occurred to me that she would simply drop dead and live no more. I had written the script of my mother's demise in my head. We would finally have all those conversations that had been avoided for years. I would listen to my mother's joys and regrets and resentments, and I would bare my soul to her as well. Then I could hold her hand and let her go with love. But, God had different plans, and I was pissed. I didn't see that as being self- centered, or that I was trying to play God. I was twenty years sober.

After my mother passed, I was afraid of drinking. After months of consciously seeking some serenity and acceptance, the opportunity to grieve and to heal was presented. God truly did for me what I could not do for myself.

Those sand dollars, those "fruits de mer," provided the lesson and the relief from despair. Was it the direct result of that conscious contact with a Higher Power? Yes. At that moment, the God of my understanding was audible, easily heard, and full of love. The power to carry that message was given to me in story, a medium that lets "me be a channel of Thy peace." When the Divine Spirit comes through us in love and in service, we have a responsibility to reach out into the world with love, and move on to Step Twelve.

∼

Exploring Spirituality and Connection With a Higher Power

1.   Right after the story is told, have participants write or sketch their response/reaction to the story, encouraging them to verbalize how they relate to it.

2.   Take participants through a guided meditation, or guided imagery, to have an experience of meditation. (There are many good ones available online that may be used.) Participants can respond to the exercise by journaling, drawing, or paired sharing.

3.   The 'fruits de mer" in this story are small items found

while walking the beach.

Often people with bring home a memento or souvenir from a trip or an event to help remember the experience. What tokens have you collected? What memories do they evoke?

4. Native Americans, and other cultures believe that totem is a spirit being, a sacred object or a symbol believed to offer protection and guidance through this life and the next. Certainly, the starfish, the whelk shell, and the sand dollars in this story were meaningful symbols of family that symbolized the circle of life. Most often, the totems are animals, who move in and out of our lives depending on the tasks that we need to complete. Have participants identify those animals to whom they are drawn or feel a connection. Participants can create a totem pole using multimedia, collage, or drawings.

5. Invite participants to share their how they see/perceive their Higher Power.

6. Give participants an envelope to address to themselves. Then ask them to write themselves a letter from their Higher Power, put it in the envelope and seal it. Collect the envelopes and send the letters several days or weeks after the session.

~

For the Storyteller

As this is my personal story, it should probably be told in first person. Please ask for permission and give credit when you tell it (and any duplication or reprint is not allowed). You may contact me at beth.ohlsson@gmail.com

~

Synopsis of story

A woman is in the process of grieving her mother. She returns three times to a beach, the site of childhood vacations and happy memories. Each time, the sea makes available a baby sea creature, which can be taken home and cherished. That these tokens are babies is not lost on this grieving woman. This spiritual experience affirmed that the circle of life requires birth, death, and rebirth, a complete and perfect cycle.

As an addendum to this story, a baby was born into this woman's extended family the day after her mother passed, and became her mother's namesake, manifesting the rebirth component of circle of life.

~

Optional Stories

"The Dream Giver." Wilkinson, Bruce, David Kopp, and Heather Harpham Kopp. *The Dream Giver*. Sisters, OR.: Multnomah Publishers, 2003.

"Sophia and the Heartmender." Olofsdotter, Marie. *Sophia and the Heartmender*. Jackson, TN: Holy Cow! Press, 1993.

John Newton and the story of "Amazing Grace"

Forest, Heather. *Wisdom Tales from Around the World Fifty Gems of Story and Wisdom from Such Diverse Traditions As Sufi, Zen, Taoist, Christian, Jewish, Buddhist, African, and Native American.* Little Rock, AR: August House Publishing, 1996.

Note: An online search will often lead to a printed version of the text of the above stories.

 **NOTES**

∼ NOTES ∼

THE TWELFTH STEP

Having had a spiritual awakening as the result of these steps,
we tried to carry the message to alcoholics,
and practice these principles in all our affairs.

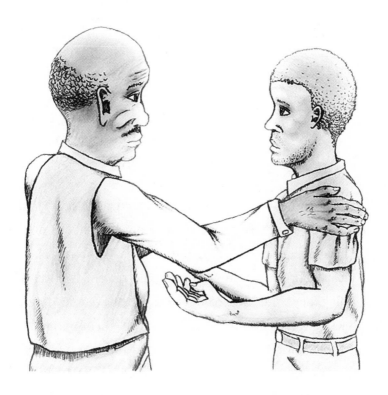

THE TWELFTH STEP HAS THREE DISTINCT PARTS. "Having had a spiritual awakening as the result of these steps …" suggests the Twelve Steps lead one to a faith that sustains a person through both the best and the worst of times. The second part of the step, "carrying the message," indicates that service to others enhances one's own spiritual life. Recovery is taught, not bought, one person at a time, one story at a time, and one day at a time. "Practicing the principles in all our affairs," entreats us to take our recovery out into the world, living in the world as we know it, as sober people with integrity and scruples. Recovering people owe it to themselves to wear their recovery proudly as they move back into the mainstream of life, as equal partners and full participants in the mainstream of life.

THE GIFT
A Blending of Two Traditional Tales
To Illustrate Step Twelve

It was Thursday night. An elderly man made his way to the church on the corner. He unlocked the door, and flipped on the light. The smoke-stained ceiling tiles had finally been replaced. New tables and chairs were neatly stacked against the wall. He was hoping they would be already set up. One by one, he dragged the tables to the center of the room and set them upright. He dragged the chairs two by two and placed them neatly around the tables. He set up the coffee pot and started it brewing. It was a familiar ritual that he enjoyed. Soon, the welcoming smell of the coffee filled the room. The old man stood with hands in pockets, and surveyed the space. He had seen miracles happen here. He'd watched as people put their lives and their families back together. Better yet was seeing the sparkling eyes of a newcomer who had come back to life with new enthusiasm.

Something very powerful happened here. He had seen it time and time again. He knew it had little to do with him, and everything to do with some power greater than all of them. He had seen that power in his own life, and had come to rely on it. Smiling to himself, he pulled two objects out of his pocket, his AA medallion with the XXII, and a large ruby that had been passed to him by his grandfather. Both were precious possessions that he carried with him, as a reminder of what mattered to him … his sobriety and his family.

A young man, sober a couple of years, burst through the door, irritable and discontent. "Can I talk to you? My sponsor said I should. I'm not liking this sober thing. I thought I would. For a while, it was exciting. But now? I am finally off probation. I got a job, a place, a car, and car insurance. Got a girlfriend. Got a sponsor. Worked the Steps, got a home group. And… and … well … NOW what? So what, I'm sober!"

"Son, what are you looking for? A medal? A gold star? A pat on the back?"

"I don't know. I guess I'm looking for some kind of reward. I want people to notice. I want this to mean something. My sponsor sent me to you. So, whatcha got?"

The old-timer put his hand into his pocket and felt the familiar shapes of the ruby and his medallion. The medallion had to be earned. But the ruby … was a gift. This ruby had to be fifty carats, exquisitely cut and faceted. It was the color of candied apples. The old-timer reached for the young man's hand, and placed the ruby into his palm. "My grandfather gave me this. I think of him every time I pull it out of my pocket. When he gave it to me, he told me he was proud of me. Here. Take it. You earned it."

"Really?… You messin' with me?" The old-timer smiled and shook his head. "Son, it's all yours."

"Awesome!" The young man rushed out of the church and down the street, completely forgetting he could have stayed for the meeting. He began to ponder this latest sober adventure. This was exciting! "Wow. If I pawned this sucker, I'd never have to worry about money!" Then he began to itemize the things he would buy and do. And then something happened. Suddenly, he felt icky. A voice inside his head whispered, "Dude, what are you doin'? You keep thinking like that, you'll get high before long." He took that in. "Maybe I'm supposed to save it so that I won't ever have to worry. It will only grow in value, and it can be my nest egg." While that thought wasn't entirely satisfactory, it wasn't entirely unsettling either. The young man went about the business of living for several days without thinking about the ruby.

One morning, the young man bolted up out of a deep sleep and realized that he didn't want the ruby. He was looking for something else. Not knowing what "it" was, he couldn't wait until Thursday, when he could talk to that old-timer again. The next Thursday, the young man walked into the basement of the church on the corner, approached the older man, grabbed his hand, and deposited the ruby in his palm.

"Don't want the ruby?"

"Nope. I want to know how you could give something away that was so precious to you."

The old-time smiled. "Because someone did that for me." The young man shook his head. "Did what?"

"There were men who took me under their wing when I first got here. They didn't just teach me about being sober. They taught me about life. Then they told me, "You got to give it away to keep it.""

"What the hell does that mean?"

"It means I can't help them, I can't pay them back. Hell, most of them are dead. But I can help you."

Exasperated, the young man mumbled, "I don't get it."

"Then let me tell you a story. Imagine a magnificent hotel ballroom, with a huge crystal chandelier high overhead. In your mind's eye, see the long banquet tables covered in fine linen tablecloths, set with fine china, crystal, and silver. Large candelabras holding multiple candles creating the warmest ambiance are on every table. Every delicacy known to man has its place on the table ... just for the taking. The men are impeccably dressed in beautifully tailored tuxedos and perfectly groomed. The women are clad in designer ball gowns, hair impeccably coiffed, with jewels dripping from their fingers and ears. They are gaunt and miserable because their arms are permanently bent at the elbow, and they cannot get the long-handled spoons to their mouths. In the midst of perfection and plenty, there is hunger and want."

"God, that's awful! That's gotta be Hell," observed the young man.

"It was. And I suspect you know all about starving in an abundant world. Now, imagine a magnificent hotel ballroom, with a huge crystal chandelier high overhead. In your mind's eye, see the long banquet tables covered in fine linen tablecloths, set with fine china, crystal, and silver. See the large candelabras holding many candles creating the warmest ambiance are on every table. Every delicacy known to man has its place on the table ... just for the taking. The men are impeccably dressed in beautifully tailored tuxedos and perfectly groomed. The women are clad in designer ball gowns, hair impeccably coiffed, with jewels dripping from their fingers and ears. But their arms are permanently bent at the elbow, and they are unable to maneuver the long-handled spoons to get the food to their mouths. Still, they all look happy and well fed. For you see, they have learned to feed each other. And that is heaven."

By now the room was filling with people arriving to attend the meeting. The young man was silent, lost in thought. The old man got up and stood near the door. The young man watched, as the old-timer extended his hand and welcomed each and every person. The welcome was genuine, put people at ease, made a difference. There was a moment when it all became clear. That old guy had been sober for decades! Reaching out and passing it on gave the old man purpose, and a reason to stay sober. Connecting with the newcomers and the relationships he had with the others put meaning into that old guy's life.

The young man began to observe what was really going on in that room, and decided to stay for the meeting. He pitched in to clean up, and then offered a ride to a newcomer who had said he needed one. Before he left, he found the old-timer and extended his hand, looking right into his eyes. There was nothing that needed to be said beyond the recognition that one recovering person helping another made all the difference. "I'm proud of you," said the old- timer as he gave the young man that pat on the back. When the young man heard the very words he had been longing to hear, he didn't know what to say. "Son, take that newbie home." The young man and the newcomer went to the car. The old-timer flipped out the light, locked the door, and headed home with very full heart.

~

Discussion of "The Gift"
As it Applies to the Twelfth Step

It has been said that religion is for people who don't want to go to hell, and spirituality is for those who have already been there. When people first come to recovery, it is rarely joyfully or willingly. It's the only option after having been to hell and back. In the process of working the Steps, one comes to a "spiritual awakening," a faith that sustains recovery and makes life worth living. The Twelve Step fellowships now have worldwide memberships through the simple act of "passing it on" one person at a time. It is a "We" program. "We" stay clean and sober, but "I" will get drunk or high.

Twelfth Step work is about carrying the message, being part of a fellowship, a community of people, who rely on their shared strength and shared commitment to maintain a quality of life that is only possible in sobriety. The sharing of personal stories is at the heart of the Twelve Step culture and tradition. "Heaven and Hell" is a familiar parable which is embedded in the story as a metaphor for addiction and recovery. In the hell of active addiction, all the abundance of the world is within reach. The alcoholic/addict just can't seem to grasp it. Recovery doesn't change the world, it changes us. It is the gift of service, and using our experience to benefit others, that brings purpose, happiness, and well-being to our lives. Recovery doesn't happen inside a Twelve Step meeting. Recovery happens outside the meetings in the way we connect with others, the way we make a positive difference, and the way we live. Wear your recovery with grace, joy, and confidence. The world needs you to do just that.

～

Exploring the Concept of Service

1. Draw your response to this story. (Remember, the quality of the artwork is irrelevant.)

2. Respond to the illustration. What thoughts and feelings does the picture evoke?

3. What would you do if someone gave you a fifty carat ruby, or an equally priceless gift?

Would it be a trigger for relapse?

4.   The paradox in the story is "You have to give it away to keep it." How does the old timer in the story explain it? Why does the old timer pay it forward? Define "paradox" and discuss those paradoxes that are familiar.

5.   Discuss the concept of service. List ways that one could be of service to one's family, or community. Explore the motivations that drive people to want to serve others, whether in a job, an organization, a cause, a project. Explore the benefits of serving others.

6.   When does serving others cross the line into self-sacrifice? What's the difference between a hero and a martyr? When and how does a person become a martyr in the name of serving others?

7.   Are members of Twelve Step Fellowships required to be of service? Does a person have to sponsor others to do Twelfth Step work? Is Twelfth step work limited to people seeking recovery or in recovery?

~

For the Storyteller

The original story for the Twelfth Step was "The Long Handled Spoons," a traditional allegory found in many cultures. The shortest version I've found is in *Dante's Inferno* which was too short to give the ending of the book the punch it needed. I heard David Claunch tell "The Ruby" as an umbrella story, framing his story about the history of Alcoholics Anonymous. It was a perfect Twelfth Step story. "The Ruby," as told by Jim May, can be found in *More Ready to Tell Tales,* by David Holt and Bill Moody, August House Publishers, 2000. "The Gift" is a blending of these two tales, illustrating the Twelfth Step and how it manifests in the recovery community.

~

Synopsis of the stories

"The Long Handled Spoons" is an allegory illustrating the difference between heaven and hell. To all appearances, the two locations are the same, but they are not. In Hell, the people cannot bring the long-handled spoons to their mouths. Consequently, they are starving and miserable. In Heaven, they have learned how to feed each other, so that all are happy and well fed.

"The Ruby" is a large, precious gemstone that a yogi bestows upon a young student.

That student ponders the gift, and hands it back stating, "I don't want that. I want what you have that allowed you to give the ruby to me."

~

Optional Stories

"The Long Handled Spoons." (Traditional).

"The Ruby." (Hindi). Holt, David, and Bill Mooney. More *Ready-to-Tell Tales.* Little Rock, AR: August House Publishing, 2000.

"The Burning of the Rice Fields." (Japan). Bryant, Sarah Cone, ed. *How to Tell Stories to Children and Some Stories to Tell.* London: George G. Harrap & Co. LTD., 1918.

"How Bridget Fed the Poor." (Ireland). Meade, Erica Helm. *The Moon in the Well: Wisdom Tales to Transform your Life, Family, and Community.* Chicago, IL: Open Court, 2001.

"Stone Soup." Forest, Heather, and Susan Gaber. *Stone Soup.* Little Rock, AR: August House LittleFolk, 2000.

Compestine, Ying Chang, and Stéphane Jorisch. *The Real Story of Stone Soup.* New York, NY: Dutton Children's , 2007.

Note: An online search will often lead to a printed text of the above stories.

∼ NOTES ∼

∼ NOTES ∼

THE THIRTEENTH STEP

NEWCOMERS ARE OFTEN STARVING FOR ATTENTION, acceptance, approval, and love. A person with some significant length
of sobriety may approach that newcomer under the pretense of
working the Steps. However, working the Steps may not be the real
agenda. Maybe sex is the real agenda. The needy and unsuspecting
newcomer embraces that person because they "really understand
me, and this is really helping me work on my sobriety," and they
are really taken in, only to be used and abused. This scenario is
referred to as the Thirteenth Step.

This 13th Step is a part of Twelve Step legend and culture,
but it does not exist in the literature of the Twelve Step Fellowships. It is a caution to the newcomer that not everyone who
attends a Twelve Step meeting is interested in living the lifestyle
of recovery. When a newcomer falls into the arms of someone
whose motives are questionable, the end result is often a relapse.
Many times those who are duped into compromising themselves
and their sobriety flee from the rooms of the Twelve Step Fellowships, never to return. We can only hope that they are sober and
safe from harm.

THE BRAHMAN GIRL WHO MARRIED A TIGER
A folktale from India

In a small village north of the Vindhya Mountains that
divide India, there was, and there was not, a Brahman woman
who defied the Hindu teachings of her people. She cared not for
prayer or meditation or any other spiritual discipline. She only
wanted what was beautiful, what she could see or touch or smell

that gave her immediate pleasure. She had to have saris of the finest silks, sandals made of gazelle leather, obsidian encased in silver, and garnets wrapped in gold circling her wrists. Her attention was easily diverted by glittering objects, flashes of color, the scent of manly sweat. Oblivious to caste and custom, her eyes strayed from one man to the next. Her heart was not far behind; yearning for each beautiful man she saw .... and the next ... and the next, causing great concern to her father, a Hindu scholar. His daughter's attachments to things, and to desires of the flesh, were an assault on Brahman teachings.

Father and mother alike were puzzled over their daughter's peculiar attitudes and behaviors, and tried to guide their offspring to better choices.

Cradled between the mountains and the village was the tiger's lair. The tiger was often drawn to the edges of the village, where he could smell palak paneer, stuffed parathas, or Alu Ki Tikki being prepared in the temple kitchens. Spicy scents of coriander, curry, cinnamon, and cardamom, mixed with onion and garlic made his mouth water in anticipation. Because of his fondness for "people-food," the tiger learned to appear as elderly Brahman farmer taking his meal at the temple's public tables. This shape-shifting was an arduous process, and each time the tiger went through the ordeal just to taste the humans' food, he vowed to take a Brahman wife to save himself the trouble.

One day, the tiger heard gossip about the girl who fell in love with every beautiful boy she saw. Grabbing a stuffed parathas for breakfast, he wandered the streets and listened closely to gather details that might prove useful. As the tiger moved through the marketplace, he looked and he listened until he found the girl who had been the subject of such gossip. Such a beauty! No wonder she wanted a beautiful boy to love and to marry. An ugly man would never do.

The next morning, the tiger assumed the shape of a beautiful Brahman teacher, proficient in all the Hindu teachings, especially the Ramayana. He broke his fast at the temple, and then stationed himself between the temple and the sacred river. He scattered holy ashes all over his body and began to read. As soon as his voice took flight on the wind, women of all ages began to gather. "The voice of the new teacher is so inviting! Let's go and listen."

After a handful of women gathered at the sacred river, the beautiful Brahman girl came to bathe in the sacred river. When the tiger caught a glimpse of her out of the corner of his eye, his rich voice increased its passion and volume to catch the girl's attention. She moved as if in a trance toward him and took her seat among the others. The tiger's eyes cast a gaze so strong she could not avert her eyes. As soon as their eyes met, she was under his spell. She felt sensations all over her body that were new and exciting. When the tiger released the girl from his gaze, she lost no time finding her mother. She pointed out the Brahman teacher as her new beloved. Her mother wasted no time finding her husband who was relieved and elated that their parenting karma had been good. He gave thanks and immediately invited the young teacher to feast with them.

There was a formal dinner to honor the new teacher, during which the father inquired about the teacher's home, parentage, and plans for the future, and pressed the young man to declare his intentions. With great warmth and great imagination, the tiger told the parents exactly what they wanted to hear. As the daughter was growing older and less desirable by the minute, the wedding took place the next day. The wedding feasts lasted for thirty days, during which the bridegroom was introduced to the family, the extended family, and the entire village. There were also thirty nights during which the bride took delight in her husband. Of course, everyone had assumed him to be human. He doted on his beautiful wife, careful to let his fingertips caress her when he walked past. This simple gesture was magic, sending warmth and excitement all over her body, keeping her spellbound. His cunning allowed him to be gracious and accommodating. His love of Brahman food and the zeal with which he devoured every dish made him a welcome guest. Surely this was a blessed match.

After thirty days of feasting, the bridegroom was longing for meat. … red meat. To eat as a human for days, or even a week, was a treat to the palette. But to deny his birthright as a mighty hunter, to deny himself the satisfaction of a tender baby elephant for lunch was more than he could bear. The bridegroom approached his father-in-law. "I have loved every moment with my lovely wife and her family. But it is time for me to return home. My parents are aging, and depend on me. They need me. I have been away too long. Please forgive me. I don't mean to be ungracious." The father-in-law was understanding, but reluctant to see the young man leave so soon after the wedding. "Of course you're reluctant to see me go. It would demand that you pay for me to travel back to this village to claim my bride and take her to her new home. I would not dream of having you go to that expense! No, my father. I will take her with me, to her future home and then turn her over to her mother-in-law. You have my assurance and my word that she will be well cared for."

It was a reasonable plan. Preparations began in earnest at sunrise. Stuffed parathas were prepared and wrapped in fresh muslin. Margosa leaves were placed on the bride's head and in her bundles to ward off demons. The family wanted assurances that their beloved child be allowed to rest when there was shade, and eat whenever they found water. The tiger agreed, and so they began their journey.

The man-tiger and his human wife walked for about an hour. The conversation was pleasant. They approached a pond, where birds sang. She asked to stop and eat. The man-tiger's response was, "Be quiet, or I'll show you my original shape." There was an edge to his words that cut her like a knife. She kept silent and kept walking. After another several hours, they approached a second pond. She asked to stop and eat. His response was the same.

Now, she wasn't just hurt. She was afraid, angry, and very hungry. "Show me. Show me your original shape."

Before she completed the second sentence, her husband's form changed. Not two legs, but four. As the front legs reached for the ground, a tail grew, and the head morphed into a tiger's face, jaws open wide and roaring at her. The horror of that transformation registered on the bride's face, and her screams matched the tiger's roar. "Know henceforth, that I, your husband, am the very tiger that speaks to you now. I can speak to you in human voice and understand every word you say. I can hear your thoughts, so be pure in thought as well as action. If you value your life, you will obey every command, and do so with respect."

Terror overtook the bride. Her movements became stiff and disjointed. Her knees were weak with fear. The tiger continued. "In an hour or so, we will reach my lair, and you will be its mistress. There are a dozen tubs, which you must fill with Brahman dishes every day. I shall make sure that you have all the ingredients that you need. You must not eat until I have had my fill." The girl wept for the rest of the journey, moving as if in a trance.

When they reached the tiger's lair, he departed quickly to hunt the flesh he craved.

Hours later, the tiger returned with the carcass of a gazelle and some pumpkins, which the bride made into a curry that satisfied him. After licking his face and paws with great satisfaction, the tiger informed her that this would be her life. Then, he settled into a well-deserved rest. As soon as he awoke, he left to hunt. Thus began the married life of the beautiful Brahman girl.

If the food pleased the tiger, he would shift into the shape of the Brahman teacher, speak kindly to her, and caress her until her body quivered in anticipation. She would close her eyes and indulge in that fantasy, soaring to heights of erotic bliss. After many days, the wife had a son, which turned out to be a tiger. The disappointment and misery made her weep constantly.

One day, while the tiger's wife was crying audibly, a crow flew into the lair and began weeping with her in earnest. Having a willing audience, she poured out her misery to the crow and asked, "Can you help me?"

"Yes," said the crow. She believed that the crow had been human in another life, and knew what needed to be done. The wife wrote her troubles with an iron nail on a palmyra leaf, begging her brothers to come rescue her. She tied the leaf to the crow's neck and entreated the crow to fly to her family home and deliver the message. The crow did, and the brothers left as soon as they finished reading the letter. Their mother didn't even have time to pack food for the journey.

Along the way, the brothers acquired a donkey, a big iron tub, and a large palmyra tree, thinking they might be of some use in their sister's rescue. Following the description in their sister's letter, they found the tiger's lair. Their sister saw them coming, and ran with outstretched arms to meet them. "The tiger will be coming home soon. You must hide in the loft and wait until he is gone. Go!" The three brothers, with the donkey, iron tub, and palmyra tree, climbed into the loft and waited.

When the tiger caught the scent of humans coming from the lair, he approached with caution. Seeing no one but his wife and his son, the tiger began to growl, and then let out a mighty roar. Startled, the donkey began to bray. The brothers began to pound on the iron tub with the tree and the racket caught the tiger off guard. "Is that an army? Preparing to wage war … against me?" The brothers continued pounding the iron tub, and the donkey kept braying.

The tiger cowered and began backing out of the lair. As the sounds intensified, the tiger bristled. The pounding and braying downed the tiger's roar. Terrified, the tiger ran away.

Wishing to take advantage of the moment, the brothers demanded they leave quickly. There was, however, the problem of the tiger cub who was asleep. Rage and the need to survive took over. The wife tore the cub into two, suspended the flesh over the hearth, and headed towards home.

When the tiger returned, he found his son being roasted. Rage and the desire for revenge took over. He vowed to roast his wife in many small pieces, not just two. How to bring her back? The tiger shifted his shape into that beautiful Brahman teacher and made his way to the village.

The family quickly made preparations to give the appearance of a hospitable welcome for their son-in-law. Not wanting to arouse concern, the mother-in-law issued an invitation for an oil bath to the man-tiger, as this was customary for honored guests. The brothers had laid thin sticks and a fine mat over a ruined well to make it appear the site of the bath. The tiger became the doting husband so he would not raise suspicion, and was led by his smiling wife to the mat. When the tiger sat on the mat, the sticks gave way, and the tiger fell down the well. The family filled the well with rocks. Thus, the tiger was prevented from doing any more mischief with beautiful, young girls.

∽

Discussion of "The Brahman Girl who Married a Tiger" As it Relates to the Thirteenth Step

This story is a warning to the newcomer to use caution when it comes to romantic relationships during early recovery. While there is no such caution in the literature, newcomers are generally advised to avoid getting into a relationship during the first year. The first year is often tumultuous, with dramatic growth changes that occur as the result of working a recovery program. This can produce anxiety, uncertainty, and loneliness as one leaves the old lifestyle behind and establishes him/her self as a sober person. During this transition, it is normal to feel vulnerable while experiencing significant change and growth.

There have been times when a man or woman familiar with the fellowship befriended a vulnerable newcomer of the opposite sex. Grateful for the positive attention from someone older either in sobriety or in years, the newcomer falls into that relationship. The flirtations start, and the newcomer is thrilled for the attention. It can begin innocently with a ride to or from the meeting, or a cup of coffee afterward. Then private meetings outside of the Twelve Step meetings begin, under the guise of doing step work or supporting the newcomer's recovery.

Before anyone realizes, the newcomer has fallen for the elder. Perhaps it's love. Perhaps it is lust. Nonetheless, that relationship provides an escape for the newcomer from the past that they now have to face. Sex can become the primary drug of choice, as can other behaviors. Sadly and too often, the newcomer relapses, caught in the revolving door of relapse and abstinence. Sometimes they flee from the room in shame. Sometimes the newcomer doesn't return.

The Brahman girl of the story falls into a similar trap, seduced by the appearance of a gentle, learned man who has bestowed his affections on her. Spellbound, she follows him into his lair, only to become a slave to all of his appetites, without benefit of affection, conversation, or appreciation. The Brahman girl is much like the newcomer, drawn to what looks good, without the perception or skill to look beneath the surface. Like the Brahman girl, the newcomer is starving for some gesture of kindness. "We'll love you until you can love yourself," is a balm to the wounded soul. The newcomer steps tentatively into that embrace, expecting to be safe.

The tiger, a predator in the animal kingdom, ventures into the world of the humans. He is there simply to have his appetites satisfied. There is no thought of how his actions will affect his bride. He simply wants what he wants, and will do anything to have it. There is no safety for those about him, as he shifts his shape to suit his own needs. Unfortunately, there are people like that everywhere; waiting to see what fate will send their way. They are charming and manipulative, casting a spell or a net in the direction of the most vulnerable.

The heroine of the story does find a way to cry for help, which is so difficult for the newcomer. She reaches out, and is able to send a message to her family who do come to her. This is not always the case for the newcomer, as the family may have had to turn their backs on the alcoholic/addict. The Brahman wife does take violent action to free herself from the trap of her marriage, but she must in order to survive. For the newcomer in the Twelve Step fellowships, cutting off old people, places, and things feels like a violent action. Saying, "No," feels like a violent action. Reaching out can be challenging, if not downright terrifying.

Newcomers have difficulty trusting themselves and their own perceptions. So if someone indicates, "I have your best interests at heart," do they really? Are they trustworthy? And is everyone in that room really working a program?

Not everyone who attends meetings is there to recover from active addiction. There are as many reasons to attend, as many reasons to get sober, as there are people in the rooms. My observation is that people generally fall into one of four categories. There are the people who are there to look good and impress someone. Then there are the people who there to get something. There are the zealots who preach the program, and make it feel like a cult. And then there are those people who are just trying to figure out this recovery lifestyle and live comfortably inside their own skin. It is this last group, those doing trying to work a program and grateful for the life they've been given, that the newcomer needs to find. People may start in one category, and move to another.

I have seen these four types of people in virtually every organization, and it takes a while to know who is who. Newcomers are well advised to be prudent and listen well. Watch people's feet as they move into the world. Trust that gut feeling, that intuition. Your antennae aren't broken. Use the intelligence you were born with. Seek out members of the same sex for guidance, unless gender preference makes that unwise. There are wonderful people in the Twelve Step Fellowships who will freely give what was given to them. Find them. They're waiting for you.

~

Examining Manipulation, Boundaries, and Self-Care

1. The Brahman girl is very taken with appearances and with high social status. What is the point of looking good? When does it become a problem? What are some of the ways people try to look good?

2. Although this story establishes the male as the predator, can the roles be reversed? The snake, another predator, is usually associated with the feminine.

3. Many times the Tiger calculates his words so that they achieve the desired effect, and delivers those words in a convincing manner. This type of manipulation is addictive behavior. When have you relied on manipulation to get what you wanted? How do you see others manipulating people or circumstances to get the desired result?

4. Often how something is said is far more important and revealing than what is said. Sarcasm, flattery, and naiveté are used to change the meaning a communication simply by changing the tone of voice. Experiment with the sentence, "Is that an army ... preparing to wage war ... against me?" See how many different messages can be conveyed with those seven words. Further experiment with, "Boy, am I

glad to see you!" "See Spot run," or "Thank you."

5. People-pleasing is a survival skill often employed by people in active addiction, as well as early recovery. In what ways does the shape-shifting tiger demonstrate that behavior?

6. The Brahman girl is the victim of domestic violence. She, like many battered partners, had great difficulty in leaving the abusive relationship, and had to resort to violence to flee the marriage. What were the cues that indicated the tiger's true stripes? Why didn't she just leave? How do you know if you're in an abusive relationship? Is it only women who become battered?

7. If the Brahman girl were tried in a court of law for the death of her spouse, what should the verdict be?

∿

For the Storyteller

When I decided to include a cautionary tale, I wanted a predator story because people need to recognize that not everyone who professes to be sober, in recovery, or interested in the newcomer's well-being isn't always being altruistic or authentic. "Bluebeard" immediately came to mind, but I wanted to go beyond the Grimm Brothers and represent cultures other than the Western European tradition. "The Brahman Girl Who Married a Tiger" is a version of the Bluebeard tale, which is AT Tale 3 Twelve. It is also similar to "The Robber Bridegroom" which is listed as AT Type

955. The original source of the story is *Tales of the Sun: Folklore of Southern India* by Mrs. Howard Kingscote and Pandit Natesa Sastri published in 1890.

∽

Synopsis

A young Hindu girl is out of control. Her parents are beside themselves as their daughter's behavior is such that a suitable match will never be made. Defying the custom of arranged marriage, the daughter falls for a handsome Brahman teacher who is really is a tiger who has shifted his shape to ensnare the girl. The parents are so grateful for this apparently good match, that they agree and spare no expense. Once married, the Tiger plots to get his bride away from her family and community, so he may exploit her to suit his own needs. Sadly, the child of that union is a tiger, and the ugly truth becomes clear. Our young bride gets word to her brothers that she needs help. They arrive, and through a ridiculous prank, are able to bring their sister home, but only after she kills the tiger cub. When the tiger realizes what has happened, he returns to his human shape to retrieve his wife. However, her family rallies behind their daughter and manipulates the tiger to an early grave.

∽

Optional Stories

"Little Red Cap" (Germany). Ragan, Kathleen, ed. *Fearless Girls, Wise Women & Beloved Sisters.* New York: W.W. Norton, 1998.

"Bluebeard" (France). Carruthers, Amelia. *Bluebeard and Other Mysterious Men with Even Stranger Facial Hair.* Cookhill, Alcester, Warwickshire: Pook Press, 2015.

"The Robber Bridegroom" (Germany). Grimm, Jacob, and Wilhelm Grimm. *The Complete Fairy Tales of the Brothers Grimm.* Trans. Jack Zipes. New York: Bantam, 1987.

"The Queen and the Murderer" (Italy). Chinen, Allan B. *Waking the World: Classic Tales of Women and the Heroic Feminine.* New York: Jeremy P. Tarcher, 1997.

"The Little Boy and His Dogs" (African American). Harris, Joel Chandler. *The Complete Tales of Uncle Remus.* Boston: Houghton Mifflin, 1983.

Note: an Internet search may lead to a printed version of the text

∿ NOTES ∿

∾ NOTES ∾

Storytelling 101

You've read this book. You've found a story you would like to tell, present, or use in some way. Now what?

Relax. You are already a storyteller. You have been telling stories your whole life, to your parents, teachers, and children, to friends and colleagues, to strangers on airplanes or metro liners, and at family get-togethers. Remember to have fun with this!

Take yourself off that hook of having to tell the story perfectly. The story is bigger than anyone in the room. Know that the story will work whether it is told or read. Trust the story to resonate with those receiving it. You really can't tell a story "wrong." Do remember that a story told is more powerful than a story read. And, you can always use the CD by the same title as this book.

Don't have an unrealistic expectation of yourself to be a performer if that's not your desire, training, vocation or avocation. Let the story be the "star."

Surrender control of the outcome of the session/class. Story is a powerful medium that helps develop empathy in the listeners which helps them mature. Once the story has been put into the space, the teller cannot, nor should not, predict what the listeners will hear, what will resonate, and what insight, or lack of same, will occur. Trust that if an issue surfaces for someone in the group, they are ready to handle it. Sanitizing the story can be counterproductive. Life is complicated, harsh, and often ugly. Stories grapple with that truth and allow the listeners to do the same.

The mechanics of learning the story are fairly simple, but will take some advance preparation. Using the synopsis of the story, identify the sequence of events. First, this happens, and then this happens, and so on. Proceed to create a storyboard from which to work. Use the steps included that follow, or do an online search for "storyboard."

To storyboard your story, draw/sketch a picture of each event. The quality of the artwork is irrelevant, trust me. Stick figures work just fine. They are my preference because the focus stays on learning the story rather than illustrating it. One drawing per page is best. Use the drawings like they were index cards, and tell the story by describing drawings in order. Practice in the privacy of your home until you are comfortable with the basic plot. The details will naturally come into the story the more you tell it. You can even take your sketches into the group or classroom to help you stay on track, much like one might use an outline or notes. This storyboard technique is used by the most seasoned professionals and is quite effective.

This volume contains twelve stories with which to play, and no further research is required. Please try telling at least one of the stories. You might find that you really enjoy this exercise as a creative process, and want to do more. The bibliography for this book has sources and resources for finding other stories that can be useful for any setting or occasion.

In therapeutic and educational settings, we often encourage and empower our charges to go beyond their comfort zones. I'm encouraging you to do the same. Have fun!

Acknowledgements

This book would not have been written without the help and support so many. Rob Coker and Perry Gaidurgis, my writing partners, thank you for believing in this project, prodding me to go deeper, and seeing me through the peaks and valleys of bringing it into the world. Shea Geremia and Mike Finley, thank you for the sensitivity you brought to your illustrations. Susan Gordon and Elizabeth Ellis, thank you for the many years of teaching, coaching, and support that led to this book. Brandt Cooper, thank you for keeping me grounded through it all.

Many thanks to Ted Parkhurst, Parkhurst Brothers Publishers, Suzanna Mallow, AMI Studios, and Kim Weitcamp, TreeHouse Artists, for bringing this body of work into the world with a passion and commitment equal to my own.

Sources for Stories

Abrahams, R. D. (Ed.). (1983). *African Folktales: Traditional Stories of the Black World.* NY: Pantheon Books.

E., & Ortiz, A. (1984). *American Indian Myths and Legends.* New York: Pantheon Books.

Andersen, H. C., Hersholt, J., & Kredel, F. (1949). *The Complete Andersen: All of the 168 Stories by Hans Christian Anderson.* New York: Heritage Press.

Barchers, S. I., & Mullineaux, L. (1990). *Wise Women: Folk and Fairy Tales from Around the World.* Libraries Unlimited Incorporated.

Bennett, W. J. (1996). *The Book of Virtues: A Treasury of Great Moral Stories.* New York: Simon & Schuster.

Bjurstrom, C. G. (Ed.). (1989). *French Folktales.* NY, NY: Pantheon Books.

Bryant, S. C. (Ed.). (1918). *How to Tell Stories to Children and Some Stories to Tell.* London: George G. Harrap & Co. LTD.

Carruthers, A. (2015). *Bluebeard and Other Mysterious Men with Even Stranger Facial Hair.* Cookhill, Alcester, Warwickshire: Pook Press.

Chase, Richard, ed. *The Jack Tales: Folk Tales from the Southern Appalachians: Collected and Retold by Richard Chase* NY: Houghton Mifflin Company, 1943.

Chinen, A. B. (1997). *Waking the World: Classic Tales of Women and the Heroic Feminine.* New York: Jeremy P. Tarcher.

Chinen, A. B. (2003). *Once Upon a Midlife: Classic Stories and Mythic Tales to Illuminate the Middle Years.* Bloomington, IN: Xlibris.

Compestine, Y. C., & Jorisch, S. (2007). *The Real Story of Stone Soup.* New York, NY: Dutton Children's Books.

Dasent, G. W. (2001). *Popular Tales from Norse Mythology.* Mineola, NY: Dover Publications.

Erdoes, R. (1998). *Legends and Tales of the American West.* New York: Pantheon Books.

Estés, C. P. (1995). *Women Who Run with the Wolves: Myths and Stories of the Wild Woman Archetype.* New York: Ballantine Books.

Forest, H. (1996). *Wisdom Tales from Around the World Fifty Gems of Story and Wisdom from Such Diverse Traditions As Sufi, Zen, Taoist, Christian, Jewish, Buddhist, African, and Native American.* Little Rock, AR: August House Publishing.

Forest, H., & Gaber, S. (2000). *Stone Soup.* Little Rock, AR: August House LittleFolk.

Franz, M. V. (1993). *The Feminine in Fairy Tales.* Boston, Mass: Shambhala.

Friedman, A., & Gilliland, J. H. (1995). *The Spectacular Gift and Other Tales from Tell Me a Story.* Kansas City, MO: Andrews and McMeel.

Glassie, H., ed. (1985). *Irish Folk Tales.* NY : Pantheon Books.

Goble, P. (1984). *Buffalo Woman.* NY: Atheneum Books.

Grimm, J., & Grimm, W. (1987). *The Complete Fairy Tales of the Brothers Grimm* (J. Zipes, Trans.). New York: Bantam.

Harris, J. C. (1983). *The Complete Tales of Uncle Remus.* Boston: Houghton Mifflin.

_____ (2008). *The Classic Tales of Brer Rabbit.* D. Daily, ed. Philadelphia, London: Courage Books an imprint of Running Press.

Holt, D., & Mooney, B. (2000). *More Ready-to-Tell Tales.* Little Rock, AR: August House Publishing.

Jacobs, J. (1892). *Celtic Fairy Tales.* Selected and edited by Joseph Jacobs, London: D. Nutt.

Jones, V. V. (Trans.). (2003). *Aesop's fables.* NY: Barnes and Noble Classics.

Kornfield, J., & Feldman, C. (Eds.). (1996). *Soul Food: Stories to Nourish the Spirit and the Heart.* San Francisco: HarperSanFrancisco.

Lang, A. (1947). *Crimson Fairy Book.* Collected and edited by A. Lang. Illustrated by Ben Kutcher, etc. Longmans, Green & Co.: New York.

Lang, A. (1966). *The Brown Fairy Book.* New York, NY: McGraw-Hill.

Lang, A. (1966). *Violet Fairy Book.* NY: Dover Publications.

Martin, R. (1992). *Rough-Face Girl.* The. G.P. Putnam's Sons.

Meade, E. H. (2001). *The Moon in the Well: Wisdom Tales to Transform your Life, Family, and Community.* Chicago, IL: Open Court.

Olofsdotter, M. (1993). *Sophia and the Heartmender.* Jackson, TN: Holy Cow! Press. Parent, M., & Olivier, J.

Parent, M., & Olivier, J. (1996). *Of kings and fools: stories of the French tradition in North America.* Little Rock, AR: August House Pub.

Pearmain, E. D. (1998). *Doorways to the Soul: 52 Wisdom Tales from Around the World.* Cleveland, OH: Pilgrim Press.

Ragan, K. (1998). *Fearless Girls, Wise Women & Beloved Sisters.* New York: W.W. Norton. Schram, P.

_____(2005). *Jewish Stories One Generation Tells Another.* Lanham: Rowman & Littlefield Schram, P.

_____(2008). *The Hungry Clothes and Other Jewish Folktales.* NY: Sterling Publishing. Stone, S.

_____(2009). "King Solomon's Quest." *Storytelling Magazine,* 21(3), 7.

Wilkinson, B., Kopp, D., & Kopp, H. H. (2003). *The Dream Giver.* Portland, OR: Multnomah.

Forest, Heather., ed. (2008). *Wisdom Tales from Around the World Fifty Gems of Story and Wisdom from Such Diverse Traditions As Sufi, Zen, Taoist, Christian, Jewish, Buddhist, African, and Native American.* Little Rock, AR: August House Publishing.

Yolen, J. (2008). *Favorite Folktales from Around the World.* New York: Pantheon Books.

References for Therapeutic Uses of Story

Albert, D. H., & Cox, A. M. (2003). *The Healing Heart—Communities: Storytelling to Build Strong and Healthy Communities.* Gabriola Island, BC: New Society.

Alcoholics Anonymous. (2006) New York City: Alcoholics Anonymous World Services, Inc.

Bettelheim, B. (1976). *The Uses of Enchantment: The Meaning and Importance of Fairy Tales.* New York, Knopf, Inc.

Burns, J. E. (1999). "Archetypal Psychology and Addiction Treatment." *Lost Souls—Spring 65—A Journal of Archetype and Culture,* Spring Journal, Woodstock, Connecticut, 15-20.

Burns, J.E. (July, 1998) *The Minnesota Model in Brazil,* Unpublished Manuscript.

Retrieved from vilaserena.com.br/vent/minnmod.pdf

Campbell, J. (1973). *The Hero with a Thousand Faces.* Princeton, N.J.: Princeton University Press. (Original work published 1949)

Cox, A. (2000). Storytelling as a Journey Down the Healing Path. Diving in the Moon, 1(1), 1-5. Retrieved May 7, 2011, from healingstory. org/.../Storytelling_Journey...

Estés, C. P. (1992). *Women Who Run with the Wolves: Myths and Stories of the Wild Woman Archetype.* New York: Ballantine Books.

Franz, Marie-Luise Von. (1993) *The Feminine in Fairy Tales.* Boston, Mass: Shambhala.

Franz, M. (1996). *The Interpretation of Fairy Tales* (Rev. ed.). Boston: Shambhala

Freeman, E. (1992). "Use of storytelling with young African-American Males; Implications for Substance Abuse Prevention." *Journal of Intergroup Relations,* 19(3), 53-72.

Gordon, S. (1993). "The powers of the handless maiden." In J. Radner, (Ed.) *Feminist Messages: Coding in Women's Folk Culture,* 252-288. Urbana: University of Illinois.

Gosin, M., Marsiglia, F. F., & Hecht, M. L. (2003). "Keepin' it REAL: A

Drug Resistance Curriculum Tailored to the Strengths and Needs of Pre-adolescents of the Southwest." *Journal of Drug Education,* 33(2), 119-142.

Gottschall, Jonathan. *The Storytelling Animal: How Stories Make us human.* Boston: Mariner, 2013.

Hecht, M. L., & Miller-Day, M. (2007). "The Drug Resistance Strategies Project as Translational Research. *Journal of Applied Communication Research,* 35(4), 343-349.

Koerner, B. I. (2010, June 23). "Secret of AA: After 75 Years, We Don't Know How it Works." *Wired,* 6, 1-10. Retrieved September 22, 2010, from https://www.wired.com/2010/06/ff_alcoholics _anonymous/

Kris, B. (1997). Drug abuse prevention: school-based strategies that work. ERIC Digest, ED409316, 1-6.

Kurtz, E., & Ketcham K. (2002). *The Spirituality of Imperfection: Storytelling and the Search for Meaning* (Bantam reissue.ed). New York, N.Y. Bantam Books.

Kushner, T., Burnham, L. F., & Paterson, D. (2001). How do you make social change? *Theatre,* 31(3), 62-93. Chicago, Ill.: Open Court.

National Institute on Drug Abuse. (2006). *Preventing Drug Use Among Children and Adolescents.* Bethesda, MD.

Ohlsson, Claiborne Beth. "Traditional Story as a Tool in Substance Abuse Prevention and Treatment." Thesis. Johnson City, TN/East Tennessee State University, 2011. N.p.: 2011. http://dc.etsu.edu/cgi/viewcontent.cgi?article=2517&context=etd

Percy, A. (2008). "Moderate adolescent drug use and the development of substance use self- regulation." *International Journal of Behavioral Development,* 32(2), 451-458.

Prust, R. (2009). "Nurturing and noxious narratives: prolonged adolescence as a storytelling failure." *The Pluralist,* 4(1), 60-67.

Adverse Childhood Experiences. (n.d.). https://www.samhsa.gov/capt/ practicing-effective-prevention/prevention-behavioral-health/ adverse-childhood-experiences

"Story therapy; why it works and how to use it with your clients." Mark Tyrrell's Therapy Skills. Blog, 03 Apr. 2016. https://www.unk.com/blog/story-therapy-why-it-works/.

Schank, R. C. (1990). *Tell me a story: Narrative and intelligence.* Evanston, Illinois. Northwestern University Press.

Stallings, F. (1988). "The web of silence: storytelling's power to hypnotize." *The National Storytelling Journal*, 1, 1-35.

Tate, M. (2005, Jan.-Feb.). "Once Upon a Time Nothing Happened." *Storytelling Magazine*, 17 Issue 1, 10-11.

"Therapeutic Storytelling." Therapeutic Storytelling | Change Your View On Life | All Things Healing. http://www.allthingshealing.com/ therapeutic-storytelling.php#.WfHzwK3MxE4

Uhler, M.A., A. S., & Parkeer, Ph.D., O. V. (2002). "Treating women drug abusers: action therapy and trauma assessment." Science & Practice Perspectives, 1, 30-37.

White, MA, W. L., & LCSW, CADC, M. S. (2008). "Recovery management and people of color: Redesigning addiction treatment for historically disempowered communities." Alcoholism Treatment Quarterly, 26(3), 365-389.

References for Storytelling

Alboher, M. (2008, August 3). "5 Tips for Telling Better Stories." https://shiftingcareers.blogs.nytimes.com/2008/08/03/5-tips-for-telling-better-stories/

Cron, L. (n.d.). "Wired for Story: The Writer's Guide to Using Brain Science to Hook Readers from the Very First Sentence." http://www.barnesandnoble.com/w/wired-for-story-lisa-cron/1110792358

Ellis, E. (2012). *From Plot to Narrative: A Step-by-Step Process of Story Creation and Enhancement.* Little Rock, AR: Parkhurst Brothers.

National Storytelling Network: We Grow Storytellers. (n.d.). http://www.storynet.org/resources/howtobecomeastoryteller.html

Sawyer, R. (1990). *The way of the storyteller.* New York: Penguin Books. Storytelling. (n.d.). https://www.ted.com/topics/storytelling.

If you have benefited from this book,
we invite you to peruse the following websites:
www.bethohlsson.com
www.parkhurstbrothers.com
www.storynet.com